LANGUAGE!

The Comprehensive Literacy Curriculum

Jane Fell Greene, Ed.D.

SOPRIS WEST EDUCATIONAL SERVICES
A CAMBIUM LEARNING COMPANY

BOSTON, MA • NEW YORK, NY • LONGMONT, CO

11 12 13 14 15   HPS   13 12 11 10 09

Editorial Director: Nancy Chapel Eberhardt
Word and Phrase Selection: Judy Fell Woods
English Learners: Jennifer Wells Greene
Lesson Development: Sheryl Ferlito, Donna Lutz, Isabel Wesley
Morphology: John Alexander, Mike Minsky, Bruce Rosow
Text Selection: Sara Buckerfield, Jim Cloonan
Decodable and Independent Text: Jenny Hamilton, Steve Harmon

LANGUAGE! is a registered trademark of Sopris West Educational Services.
LANGUAGE! eReader is a customized version of the CAST eReader for
Windows ® (version 3.0). CAST eReader © 1995–2003, CAST, Inc.
and its licensors. All rights reserved.

Rube Goldberg and Rube Goldberg Machine Contest are registered trademarks of Rube Goldberg, Inc. Kevlar is a registered trademark of E. I. du Pont de Nemours and Company. Dodge and Intrepid are registered trademarks of the Daimler Chrysler Corporation. The Incredible Hulk and Iron Man are registered trademarks of Marvel Characters, Inc. Keith Haring is a registered trademark of the Estate of Keith Haring. Superman is a registered trademark of DC Comics, Inc. Olympic is a registered trademark of the U.S. Olympic Committee. Chicago Marathon is a registered trademark of the LaSalle Bank Corporation. Tony Hawk and the Tony Hawk Foundation are registered trademarks of Anthony Hawk. Brooklyn Dodgers is a registered trademark of Los Angeles Dodgers, LLC. Pittsburgh Pirates is a registered trademark of Pittsburgh Associates Limited Partnership. National League is a registered service mark of the National League of Professional Baseball Clubs. Gold Glove Award is a registered service mark of Rawlings Sporting Goods Company, Inc. Baseball Hall of Fame is a registered trademark of the National Baseball Hall of Fame and Museum, Inc. Union Pacific Railroad is a registered service mark of the Union Pacific Railroad Company.

ISBN 13 Digit: 978-1-59318-323-3
ISBN 10 Digit: 1-59318-323-2

Printed in the United States of America

Published and distributed by

Cambium
LEARNING®
Sopris West®

4093 Specialty Place • Longmont, CO 80504 • (303) 651-2829
www.sopriswest.com

70885/12-09

Table of Contents

Check off the activities you complete with each lesson. Evaluate your accomplishments at the end of each lesson. Pay attention to teacher evaluations and comments.

Unit Objectives	Lesson 1 (Date:_____)	Lesson 2 (Date:_____)
STEP 1 — **Phonemic Awareness and Phonics** • Identify closed syllables. • Identify stressed and unstressed syllables in multisyllable words. • Recognize the schwa in multisyllable words.	❑ Vowel Chart (T) ❑ Consonant Chart (T) ❑ Syllable Awareness: Segmentation	❑ Syllable Awareness: Segmentation ❑ Exercise 1: Listening for Sounds in Words
STEP 2 — **Word Recognition and Spelling** • Read and spell words with closed syllables. • Read words with shifting stress patterns. • Read and spell words with prefixes: **dis-, in-, non-, un-**. • Read and spell contractions with **am** or **is**. • Read and spell the **Essential Words**: *gone, look, most, people, see, water*.	❑ Exercise 1: Spelling Pretest 1 ❑ Memorize It	❑ Exercise 2: Listening for Word Parts ❑ Exercise 3 Sort It: Short Vowels ❑ Exercise 4: Build It ❑ Word Fluency 1 ❑ Memorize It: Essential Words ❑ Handwriting Practice
STEP 3 — **Vocabulary and Morphology** • Define **Unit Vocabulary** words. • Identify antonyms, synonyms, and attributes. • Define compound words. • Use the meaning of prefixes to define words.	❑ Unit Vocabulary ❑ Explore It (T) ❑ Expression of the Day	❑ Exercise 5: Sort It: Compound Words ❑ Compound Words: Three Kinds ❑ Exercise 6: Find It: Compound Words ❑ Expression of the Day
STEP 4 — **Grammar and Usage** • Identify and use **be** as a helping verb. • Identify nominative and object pronouns. • Identify direct object.	❑ Exercise 2: Identify It: Nouns ❑ Exercise 3: Find It: Pronouns	❑ Exercise 7: Identify It: Past, Present, and Future
STEP 5 — **Listening and Reading Comprehension** • Use context-based strategies to define words. • Identify signal words: use, generalize, infer. • Identify transition words for classification in informational text.	❑ Exercise 4: Phrase It ❑ Independent Text: "Off-the-Wall Inventions" ❑ Exercise 5: Find It: Closed Syllables	❑ Passage Fluency 1 ❑ Exercise 8: Use the Clues
STEP 6 — **Speaking and Writing** • Organize main ideas and details for writing. • Write responses to Answer It questions with the signal words: use, generalize, infer. • Use transition words for classification in paragraph development.	❑ Masterpiece Sentences: Stages 1–4 ❑ Sentence Types: Fact or Opinion?	❑ Exercise 9: Rewrite It
Self-Evaluation (5 is the highest) **Effort** = I produced my best work. **Participation** = I was actively involved in tasks. **Independence** = I worked on my own.	**Effort:** 1 2 3 4 5 **Participation:** 1 2 3 4 5 **Independence:** 1 2 3 4 5	**Effort:** 1 2 3 4 5 **Participation:** 1 2 3 4 5 **Independence:** 1 2 3 4 5
Teacher Evaluation	**Effort:** 1 2 3 4 5 **Participation:** 1 2 3 4 5 **Independence:** 1 2 3 4 5	**Effort:** 1 2 3 4 5 **Participation:** 1 2 3 4 5 **Independence:** 1 2 3 4 5

Lesson 3 (Date:_____)	Lesson 4 (Date:_____)	Lesson 5 (Date:_____)
❑ Syllable Awareness: Segmentation ❑ Exercise 1: Listening for Sounds in Words	❑ Exercise 1: Syllable Awareness: Segmentation	❑ Content Mastery: Syllable Awareness
❑ Exercise 2: Build It ❑ Exercise 3: Find It: Essential Words ❑ Word Fluency 1	❑ Exercise 2: Find It: Prefixes ❑ Exercise 3: Sort It: Prefixes ❑ Word Fluency 2 ❑ Type It	❑ Content Mastery: Spelling Posttest 1
❑ Exercise 4: Define It ❑ Draw It: Idioms ❑ Expression of the Day	❑ Exercise 4: Match It: Using Prefixes ❑ Expression of the Day	❑ Exercise 1: Word Networks: Antonyms ❑ Exercise 2: Word Networks: Synonyms ❑ Exercise 3: Word Networks: Attributes ❑ Draw It: Idioms ❑ Expression of the Day
❑ Exercise 5: Identify It: *Be*—Main Verb or Helping Verb ❑ Exercise 6: Identify It: The Verb *Be*	❑ Exercise 5: Tense Timeline (T)	❑ Masterpiece Sentences: Stages 1–3 ❑ Masterpiece Sentences: Helping Verbs
❑ Instructional Text: "It'll Never Work" (T) ❑ Exercise 7: Use the Clues	❑ Exercise 6: Blueprint for Reading: Main Ideas and Transition Words for Classification (T)	❑ Exercise 6: Blueprint for Reading: Main Ideas, Transition Words, and Details (T) (Lesson 4)
❑ Exercise 8: Answer It	❑ Introduction: Topic Sentence ❑ Exercise 7: Blueprint for Writing: Outline (T) ❑ Challenge Text: "Leonardo da Vinci: The Inventor"	❑ Exercise 7: Blueprint for Writing: Outline (T) (Lesson 4) ❑ Write It: Classification Paragraph (T) ❑ Challenge Text: "Leonardo da Vinci: The Inventor"
Effort: 1 2 3 4 5 **Participation:** 1 2 3 4 5 **Independence:** 1 2 3 4 5	**Effort:** 1 2 3 4 5 **Participation:** 1 2 3 4 5 **Independence:** 1 2 3 4 5	**Effort:** 1 2 3 4 5 **Participation:** 1 2 3 4 5 **Independence:** 1 2 3 4 5
Effort: 1 2 3 4 5 **Participation:** 1 2 3 4 5 **Independence:** 1 2 3 4 5	**Effort:** 1 2 3 4 5 **Participation:** 1 2 3 4 5 **Independence:** 1 2 3 4 5	**Effort:** 1 2 3 4 5 **Participation:** 1 2 3 4 5 **Independence:** 1 2 3 4 5

Check off the activities you complete with each lesson. Evaluate your accomplishments at the end of each lesson. Pay attention to teacher evaluations and comments.

Unit Objectives	Lesson 6 (Date:_____)	Lesson 7 (Date:_____)
STEP 1 **Phonemic Awareness and Phonics** • Identify closed syllables. • Identify stressed and unstressed syllables in multisyllable words. • Recognize the schwa in multisyllable words.	❑ Exercise 1: Listening for Stressed Syllables	❑ Introduction: Shifting the Syllable Stress ❑ Exercise 1: Listening for Stressed Syllables ❑ Introduction: Schwa ❑ Schwa in the Unstressed Syllable
STEP 2 **Word Recognition and Spelling** • Read and spell words with closed syllables. • Read words with shifting stress patterns. • Read and spell words with prefixes: **dis-, in-, non-, un-**. • Read and spell contractions with **am** or **is**. • Read and spell the **Essential Words**: *gone, look, most, people, see, water.*	❑ Exercise 2: Spelling Pretest 2 ❑ Word Fluency 3	❑ Build It: Words With Schwa ❑ Exercise 2: Contract It ❑ Exercise 3: Choose It and Use It
STEP 3 **Vocabulary and Morphology** • Define **Unit Vocabulary** words. • Identify antonyms, synonyms, and word attributes. • Define compound words. • Use the meaning of prefixes to define words.	❑ Unit Vocabulary ❑ Exercise 3: Word Networks: Antonyms, Synonyms, and Attributes ❑ Expression of the Day	❑ Exercise 4: Match It: Using Prefixes ❑ Expression of the Day
STEP 4 **Grammar and Usage** • Identify and use **be** as a helping verb. • Identify nominative and object pronouns. • Identify direct object.	❑ Exercise 4: Code It: Direct Object	❑ Exercise 5: Code It: Noun or Verb ❑ Identify It
STEP 5 **Listening and Reading Comprehension** • Use context-based strategies to define words. • Identify signal words: use, generalize, infer. • Identify transition words for classification in informational text.	❑ Exercise 5: Phrase It ❑ Independent Text: "Solving Problems" ❑ Exercise 6: Use the Clues	❑ Passage Fluency 2 ❑ Exercise 6: Use the Clues
STEP 6 **Speaking and Writing** • Organize main ideas and details for writing. • Write responses to Answer It questions with the signal words: use, generalize, infer. • Use transition words for classification in paragraph development.	❑ Exercise 7: Rewrite It	❑ Exercise 7: Rewrite It
Self-Evaluation (5 is the highest) **Effort** = I produced my best work. **Participation** = I was actively involved in tasks. **Independence** = I worked on my own.	**Effort:** 1 2 3 4 5 **Participation:** 1 2 3 4 5 **Independence:** 1 2 3 4 5	**Effort:** 1 2 3 4 5 **Participation:** 1 2 3 4 5 **Independence:** 1 2 3 4 5
Teacher Evaluation	**Effort:** 1 2 3 4 5 **Participation:** 1 2 3 4 5 **Independence:** 1 2 3 4 5	**Effort:** 1 2 3 4 5 **Participation:** 1 2 3 4 5 **Independence:** 1 2 3 4 5

Lesson 8 (Date:_____)	Lesson 9 (Date:_____)	Lesson 10 (Date:_____)
❑ Exercise 1: Listening for Stressed Syllables ❑ Vowel Chart	❑ Exercise 1: Listening for Stressed Syllables	❑ Exercise 1: Listening for Stressed Syllables
❑ Divide It ❑ Word Fluency 4	❑ Exercise 2: Build It	❑ Content Mastery: Spelling Posttest 2
❑ Content Mastery: Word Relationships ❑ Content Mastery: Prefixes	❑ Exercise 3: Find It: Compound Words and Words With Prefixes ❑ Exercise 4: Sort It: Compound Words and Words With Prefixes ❑ Exercise 5: Define It ❑ Expression of the Day	❑ Exercise 2: Sort It: Inventions (T) ❑ Draw It: Idioms ❑ Expression of the Day
❑ Diagram It (T) ❑ Exercise 2: Diagram It: Subject, Predicate, and Direct Object (T)	❑ Masterpiece Sentences: Stages 1 and 2	❑ Content Mastery: Helping Verbs ❑ Content Mastery: Nouns or Pronouns ❑ Content Mastery: Nouns and Pronouns as Direct Objects
❑ Instructional Text: "Way to Go!" ❑ Exercise 3: Use the Clues	❑ Instructional Text: "Way to Go!" ❑ Exercise 6: Answer It	❑ Exercise 3: Listening for Details
❑ Exercise 4: Answer It	❑ Write It: Topic Sentence ❑ Exercise 7: Write It: Conclusion Sentence ❑ Challenge Text: "Podway Bound: A Science Fiction Story"	❑ Exercise 4: Blueprint for Writing: Developing Main Ideas ❑ Challenge Text: "Podway Bound: A Science Fiction Story"
Effort: 1 2 3 4 5 **Participation:** 1 2 3 4 5 **Independence:** 1 2 3 4 5	**Effort:** 1 2 3 4 5 **Participation:** 1 2 3 4 5 **Independence:** 1 2 3 4 5	**Effort:** 1 2 3 4 5 **Participation:** 1 2 3 4 5 **Independence:** 1 2 3 4 5
Effort: 1 2 3 4 5 **Participation:** 1 2 3 4 5 **Independence:** 1 2 3 4 5	**Effort:** 1 2 3 4 5 **Participation:** 1 2 3 4 5 **Independence:** 1 2 3 4 5	**Effort:** 1 2 3 4 5 **Participation:** 1 2 3 4 5 **Independence:** 1 2 3 4 5

Exercise 1 · Spelling Pretest 1

▶ Write each word your teacher repeats.

1. _____   6. _____   11. _____

2. _____   7. _____   12. _____

3. _____   8. _____   13. _____

4. _____   9. _____   14. _____

5. _____   10. _____   15. _____

Exercise 2 · Identify It: Nouns

▸ Read the excerpt from **"Off-the-Wall Inventions"** below.

▸ Decide if each underlined noun names a person, place, thing, or idea.

▸ Write the noun in the correct column in the chart below.

▸ The first one is done for you. **Hint:** One of the words can be in two columns.

---

based on "Off-the-Wall Inventions"

Drive the C5

Step back in time. It is 1985. In **England**, a man makes a **bike** with
$\quad$ 1 $\qquad\qquad\qquad\qquad\qquad\qquad\qquad$ 2
3 wheels. This bike is not ridden. It's driven! C5 is its name. The
C5 has an upside; it runs on **batteries**, not gas! It does not emit gas
$\qquad\qquad\qquad\qquad\qquad$ 3
fumes. Ships use C5s. The small C5s can drive across the **decks** of
$\qquad\qquad\qquad\qquad\qquad\qquad\qquad\qquad\qquad\qquad\qquad$ 4
big ships. A C5 helps move things on a ship, but it has a downside.
If you drive the C5 in **traffic**, you will find that it's too small and
$\qquad\qquad\qquad\qquad$ 5
sluggish. Also, the **driver** is exposed. Passing cars emit gas fumes.
$\qquad\qquad\qquad\quad$ 6
The driver inhales these toxic fumes! This is quite a **problem**. Back
$\qquad\qquad\qquad\qquad\qquad\qquad\qquad\qquad\qquad\qquad$ 7
to the present. There is a contest for **students**. Students make odd
$\qquad\qquad\qquad\qquad\qquad\qquad\qquad$ 8
things. The oddest invention wins. Do you have an "off-the-wall"
plan? Invent something that makes us smile, and you might win a
9
trip to **Mars**, on a C5!
$\qquad$ 10

Persons	Places	Things	Ideas
	England		

Unit 13 · Lesson 1

Exercise 3 · Find It: Pronouns

▸ Read each sentence.

▸ Underline the pronoun.

▸ Fill in the bubble to show if the pronoun is the nominative or objective form.

▸ The first one is done for you.

	nominative	objective
1. <u>We</u> were helping Jan.	●	○
2. She was expanding the report.	○	○
3. Jane was expanding it.	○	○
4. We connected the dots.	○	○
5. The inventions amazed them.	○	○

Exercise 4 · Phrase It

▸ Use the penciling strategy to "scoop" the phrases in each sentence.

▸ Read the sentences as you would speak them.

▸ The first two are done for you.

1. Some inventions were made just for fun.

2. They are "off the wall."

3. They will not have an impact.

4. A fad is a quick craze.

5. He had invented lots of nutty things.

6. He just loves tinkering.

7. Step back in time to 1985.

8. The C5 runs on batteries, not gas.

9. It emits no gas fumes.

10. A C5 helps move things on a ship.

Unit 13 · Lesson 1

Exercise 5 · Find It: Closed Syllables

▸ Listen to your teacher read the text.

▸ Reread the text silently or quietly to yourself.

▸ Highlight **closed syllables** in words.

▸ Sort each closed syllable according to its vowel sound.

▸ Record nonphonetic words and words that you're unsure of in the last column under the "?"

> Some inventions were made just for fun. Some of them are odd.
>
> Many of them have odd names. They are just not useful. Not many
>
> of them will sell. They will not have any impact.

ă	ĕ	ĭ	ŏ	ŭ	?

Exercise 1 · Listening for Sounds in Words

▸ Listen to each word your teacher says.

▸ Identify the short vowel sound.

▸ Mark the short vowel sound with a breve (˘).

1. a   e   i   o   u
2. a   e   i   o   u
3. a   e   i   o   u
4. a   e   i   o   u
5. a   e   i   o   u
6. a   e   i   o   u
7. a   e   i   o   u
8. a   e   i   o   u
9. a   e   i   o   u
10. a   e   i   o   u

Unit 13 · Lesson 2

Exercise 2 · Listening for Word Parts

▸ Listen to each word your teacher says.

▸ Write the word part that your teacher repeats.

1. _____   2. _____   3. _____   4. _____   5. _____

6. _____   7. _____   8. _____   9. _____   10. _____

Exercise 3 · Sort It: Short Vowels

▸ Use the words and word parts from Exercise 2, **Listening for Word Parts**.

▸ Write each word or word part under the correct short vowel sound.

ă	ĕ	ĭ	ŏ	ŭ

Exercise 4 · Build It

▸ Use the answers from Exercise 2, **Listening for Word Parts**.

▸ Combine word parts to create new words.

▸ Circle the compound words.

_____   _____   _____   _____

_____   _____   _____   _____

▸ Answer the question.

How do you know the words that you circled are compound words?

_____

_____

Unit 13 · Lesson 2

Exercise 5 · Sort It: Compound Words

▸ Decide whether the parts of each compound help with the meaning.

▸ Write the word in the correct column.

▸ The first two are done for you.

Compound Word	Last Part Names the Item	Not the Sum of the Parts
Example: downhill	downhill	
Example: laptop		laptop
1. windfall		
2. fishnet		
3. clamshell		
4. hotshot		
5. wineglass		
6. smalltime		
7. upscale		
8. gemstone		
9. makeshift		
10. dishcloth		

Exercise 6 · Find It: Compound Words

▸ Use your dictionary to find compound words with **jump** and **back**.

▸ Write each word in the correct column.

Connected (Closed)	Hyphenated	Spaced Apart (Open)
Example: jumpsuit	**Example:** jump-start	**Example:** jump shot

Unit 13 · Lesson 2

Exercise 7 · Identify It: Past, Present, and Future

▸ Decide whether the underlined verb or verb phrase shows actions in the past, present, or future.

▸ Fill in the correct bubble.

▸ The first one is done for you.

	Past	Present	Future
1. They <u>will adapt</u> to their new school.	○	○	●
2. He <u>assisted</u> the small children at the bus stop.	○	○	○
3. I <u>am attaching</u> this lock to my bike.	○	○	○
4. They <u>collect</u> dozens of jackets for people.	○	○	○
5. Our campus <u>expanded</u> by over 100 students this month.	○	○	○
6. They <u>will suspend</u> bids on that project.	○	○	○
7. We <u>are finishing</u> our project this month.	○	○	○
8. They <u>will be selecting</u> a president this fall.	○	○	○
9. His lunch <u>vanished</u> in about six seconds.	○	○	○
10. We <u>are visiting</u> our granddad at his cabin.	○	○	○

Exercise 8 · Use the Clues

▸ Read the sentence pairs.

▸ Read the pronoun that is circled.

▸ Identify the noun that the pronoun is replacing in each sentence.

▸ Draw an arrow to show the link between the pronoun and the noun it replaced.

▸ Underline the noun that the pronoun is referring to.

1. Some inventions are made just for fun. Many of (them) have odd names.

2. Fads become the rage. People like (them).

3. Meet Mr. Robinson. (He) has invented lots of nutty things.

4. In England, a man is making a small 3-wheeled bike. (It) is called the C5.

5. If you drive a C5 in traffic, you'll find that (it) is too small. It's too sluggish.

Unit 13 · Lesson 2

Exercise 9 · Rewrite It

▸ Read each sentence pair in Exercise 8: **Use the Clues**.

▸ Replace the circled pronoun with the noun that it represents.

▸ Rewrite the sentence using the noun.

▸ Check for sentence signals—capital letters and end punctuation.

▸ Read the new sentence.

1. _____

2. _____

3. _____

4. _____

5. _____

Exercise 1 · Listening for Sounds in Words

▸ Listen for the short vowel sound in each word your teacher says.

▸ Write the letter for the vowel sound in the position where you hear it.

▸ Mark the vowel with a breve (ĕ) to show the sound.

1.

2.

3.

4.

5.

6.

7.

8.

9.

10.

Unit 13 · Lesson 3

Exercise 2 · Build It

▸ Combine the closed syllables in the **Word Bank** to build as many new words as possible.

Word Bank

clam	in	bot
lem	shell	vent
tom	ing	et
on	rock	ed

▸ Use the **Doubling Rule** to double the final consonant as needed.

▸ Write the words on the lines below.

_____   _____

_____   _____

_____   _____

_____   _____

Exercise 3 · Find It: Essential Words

▸ Write the sentences that your teacher dictates.

1. _____

2. _____

3. _____

4. _____

▸ Find the six **Essential Words** for this unit in the dictated sentences.

▸ Underline them. There may be more than one in a sentence.

▸ Use the *Student Text* for the list of **Essential Words**, if needed.

▸ Write the **Essential Words** on the lines.

_____   _____   _____   _____   _____   _____

Exercise 4 · Define It

▸ Fill in the blanks with a category and an attribute to define the word.

▸ If you're unsure of your definition, compare with a dictionary.

▸ Do the first two words with your teacher.

1. An **atlas** is _____ that _____

   _____.

2. A **clamshell** is _____ that _____

   _____.

3. A **fishnet** is _____ that _____

   _____.

(continued)

Exercise 4 (continued) · Define It

4. A **laptop** is _____ that _____

_____.

5. A **jacket** is _____ that _____

_____.

6. **Cotton** is _____ that _____

_____.

7. A **magnet** is _____ that _____

_____.

8. A **checklist** is _____ that _____

_____.

9. A **ticket** is _____ that _____

_____.

10. **Water** is _____ that _____

_____.

▸ Which vocabulary words above are compound words?

▸ Write the compound words on the lines.

_____   _____   _____

Exercise 5 · Identify It: *Be*—Main Verb or Helping Verb

PERSON	Past		Base Verb		Future	
	singular	plural	singular	plural	singular	plural
1st person	*(I)* was	*(we)* were	*(I)* am	*(we)* are	*(I)* will be	*(we)* will be
2nd person	*(you)* were	*(you)* were	*(you)* are	*(you)* are	*(you)* will be	*(you)* will be
3rd person	*(he, she, it)* was	*(they)* were	*(he, she, it)* is	*(they)* are	*(he, she, it)* will be	*(they)* will be

▸ Use the chart to identify the form of the verb **be** in the following sentences.

▸ Underline the form of **be** that you find.

▸ Fill in the bubble to show if the form of **be** is used as a main verb or helping verb.

	Main Verb	Helping Verb
1. We are inventors.	◯	◯
2. She was writing a report.	◯	◯
3. He will be president of his class.	◯	◯
4. You were listening to a famous song.	◯	◯
5. I am collecting cans for my project.	◯	◯

Unit 13 · Lesson 3

Exercise 6 · Identify It: The Verb *Be*

▶ Use the chart to identify the helping verb (form of **be**) in these sentences.

▶ Circle the helping verb.

▶ Fill in the bubble to show if the verb **be** is in the past, present, or future tense.

	Past	Present	Future
1. We will be collecting shells.	◯	◯	◯
2. She was expanding her report.	◯	◯	◯
3. He is connecting the segments.	◯	◯	◯
4. They were selecting the ones they liked.	◯	◯	◯
5. I am finishing the project today.	◯	◯	◯

Exercise 7 · Use the Clues

▶ Use context clues to define **multipurpose**.

▶ Underline the vocabulary word.

▶ Read text before and after the unknown word.

▶ Sometimes words or phrases are substituted with synonyms to make the text more interesting.

▶ Underline the word or words substituted for the unknown word.

▶ Draw an arrow to show the link between the unknown word and the word or words that were substituted.

---

based on "It'll Never Work"

A second unsuccessful invention was a machine with many functions. You've heard of multipurpose. One invention didn't even know what it was. Or rather, it tried to be everything. It was a car. It was a boat. It was a plane. It was all three. Too bad the idea didn't take off. And neither did the machine.

Define It

▶ Write a definition based on the context clues.

▶ Verify your definition with the dictionary or www.yourdictionary.com.

multipurpose—_____

_____

Unit 13 · Lesson 3

Exercise 8 · Answer It

▸ Underline the signal word in each question.

▸ Write the answer in a complete sentence or sentences.

▸ Check for sentence signals—capital letters and end punctuation.

1. Reread the first paragraph of **"It'll Never Work."** What can you infer about the phrase "missed the boat?"

   _____

   _____

   _____

2. What can you generalize about the types of inventions described in the section of text titled "Some Inventions That Never Took Off"?

   _____

   _____

   _____

3. Illustrate one of the inventions in the section of text titled "Strange But True: Other Unbelievable Inventions."

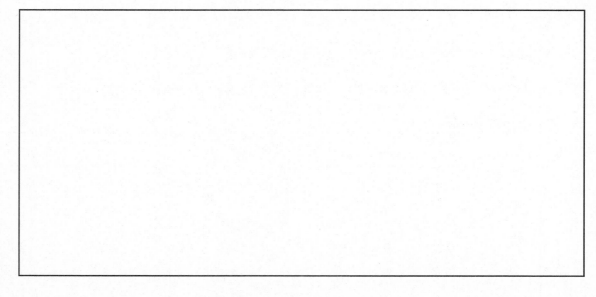

(continued)

Exercise 8 (continued) · Answer It

4. Explain the meaning of Rube Goldberg arrangements.

_____

_____

_____

5. Using the Internet address from the last paragraph of this selection, tell something new about Rube Goldberg.

_____

_____

_____

Exercise 1 · Syllable Awareness: Segmentation

▸ Listen to each word your teacher says.

▸ Count the syllables. Write the number in the first column.

▸ Write the letter for each vowel sound you hear.

▸ Mark each short vowel with a breve (˘).

	How many syllables do you hear?	First vowel sound	Second vowel sound
1.			
2.			
3.			
4.			
5.			
6.			
7.			
8.			
9.			
10.			

Exercise 2 · Find It: Prefixes

▸ Circle the prefix: **dis-**, **in-**, **un-** and **non-**.

▸ Blend the prefix and the base word to read the entire word.

nonfat	unclasp	inland	distrust
nonskid	disrupt	input	unbent
discuss	nonstick	nonstop	unplug
instep	unfit	unlock	infect

Exercise 3 · Sort It: Prefixes

▸ Sort the words from Exercise 2, **Find It: Prefixes**, by prefix.

▸ Read the words to a partner.

▸ One example of each prefix is done for you.

dis-	in-	non-	un-
distrust	inland	nonfat	unclasp

Unit 13 · Lesson 4

Exercise 4 · Match It: Using Prefixes

▸ Use what you know about the prefix, **un-**, to match the word to its definition.

▸ Draw a line to match the word with its definition.

▸ Use a dictionary to verify your answers.

Word	Definition
1. unwell	**a.** to undo the button
2. unfit	**b.** take out of a container, undo the packing
3. unpack	**c.** not, opposite
4. unbutton	**d.** not well, unhealthy, sick.
5. un-	**e.** not fit, weak

▸ Look at definitions for items 1–5. What words do they have in common?

Un- means: _____

▸ Use what you know about the prefix, **non-**, to match the word to its definition.

▸ Draw a line to match the word with its definition.

▸ Use a dictionary to verify your answers.

Word	Definition
6. nonstop	**a.** without sense, foolishness
7. nonsense	**b.** not equal
8. nontoxic	**c.** without stop, made or done without stop or stopping
9. non-equal	**d.** without, not or no
10. non-	**e.** without or not toxic, without poison(s)

▸ Look at definitions for items 6–10. What words to they have in common?

Non- means: _____

Exercise 5 · Tense Timeline

▶ Read the five sentences below.

▶ Write the verb or verb phrase under the correct position on the **Tense Timeline**.

▶ Expand the verb to include six total forms: *past, present, future, past progressive, present progressive*, and *future progressive*.

1. I **punished** my dog for digging up the garden.

Past	Present	Future

2. We **will be visiting** the museum with the other classes.

3. He **was admitting** his problem.

4. Time **is vanishing**.

5. She **connects** them with others.

Exercise 6 · Blueprint for Reading: Main Ideas and Transition Words for Classification

▸ Highlight the main idea of each paragraph in blue.

▸ Put a circle around the transition words: **One**, **A second**, **Another**, **Then**, and **A final**.

---

from "It'll Never Work"

Some Inventions That Never Took Off

One example of an unsuccessful invention was the Sinclair C5. This vehicle was supposed to solve the traffic problems in Britain. It could travel. But it went only 20 miles an hour. What was it? Actually, it was a tricycle. It was battery- and pedal-powered. And it sold. But it didn't sell well—or for long. Within two months, the C5 was defunct!

A second unsuccessful invention was a machine with many functions. You've heard of multipurpose. This invention was a strange-looking vehicle. Or rather, it tried to be everything. It was a car. It was a boat. It was a plane. It was all three. Too bad the idea didn't take off. And neither did the machine.

Another unsuccessful invention was the Spring Walker. This walking device promised to be fun. It put a spring in your step. It was supposed to be just the thing for a stroll around the park. But running for the bus could have disastrous results! A person could trip and fall!

(continued)

Then there was Piggles Takes to the Air. This invention was another transportation sensation. It was pieced together from scrap metal and an old motorcycle engine. It was created to raise money for charity. Did it work? Sure. And pigs might fly!

A final example of an unsuccessful invention was the Dynasphere. It was invented in 1932. This invention moved by using a giant wheel that turned around the driver. It sped along at nearly 30 miles per hour. One thing was in its favor. It was powered by electricity. It polluted less than other cars. Even so, it didn't exactly roll off the production line.

Exercise 7 · Blueprint for Writing: Outline

_____

I. _____

   A. _____

   B. _____

   C. _____

   D. _____

II. _____

   A. _____

   B. _____

   C. _____

   D. _____

III. _____

   A. _____

   B. _____

   C. _____

   D. _____

(continued)

Exercise 7 (continued) · Blueprint for Writing: Outline

IV. _____

    A. _____

    B. _____

    C. _____

    D. _____

V. _____

    A. _____

    B. _____

    C. _____

    D. _____

_____

Exercise 1 · Word Networks: Antonyms

▸ Read the words in the **Word Bank**.

Word Bank

under	top	uncommon
connect	stop	across

▸ Select and write the antonym (opposite) for each word your teacher says.

▸ Discuss your answers.

1. bottom _____

2. disconnect _____

3. over _____

4. nonstop _____

5. common _____

Exercise 2 · Word Networks: Synonyms

▸ Read the words in the **Word Bank**.

Word Bank

bottom	finish	vanish
random	uncommon	nonstop

▸ Select and write the synonym (same or almost the same) for each word your teacher says.

▸ Discuss your answers.

1. base _____

2. end _____

3. direct _____

4. chance _____

5. disappear _____

Unit 13 · Lesson 5

Exercise 3 · Word Networks: Attributes

▶ Read the words in the **Word Bank**.

Word Bank

soft	buttons	bottom
dozen	maps	thin

▶ Select and write the attribute (size, part, color, function) for each word your teacher says.

▶ Discuss your answers.

1. atlas _____

2. cotton _____

3. jacket _____

4. ribbon _____

5. eggs _____

Exercise 1 · Listening for Stressed Syllables

▸ Listen to the word your teacher says.

▸ Repeat the word.

▸ Listen for the stressed syllable.

▸ Make an X in the box to mark the position of the stressed syllable.

	1st Syllable	2nd Syllable
Example: pilgrim	X	
1. inflict		
2. magnet		
3. camel		
4. adapt		
5. method		

Unit 13 · Lesson 6

Exercise 2 · Spelling Pretest 2

▸ Listen to the word your teacher repeats.

▸ Write the word.

1. _____

2. _____

3. _____

4. _____

5. _____

6. _____

7. _____

8. _____

9. _____

10. _____

11. _____

12. _____

13. _____

14. _____

15. _____

Exercise 3 · Word Networks: Antonyms, Synonyms, and Attributes

▸ Read each pair of words.

▸ Sort word pairs according to their relationship.

▸ Write the word pairs in the correct column.

▸ Discuss answers with a partner.

base: bottom	bottom: top	jacket: buttons	disconnect: connect
ribbon: thin	end: finish	common: uncommon	disappear: vanish
over: above	eggs: dozen	cotton: soft	nonstop: stop

Antonyms (Opposite)	Synonyms (Same)	Attributes

Unit 13 · Lesson 6

Exercise 4 · Code It: Direct Object

▸ Draw one line under the simple subject. Code it **ss**.

▸ Draw two lines under the simple predicate. Code it **sp**.

▸ Find the direct object. Code it **do**.

                       SS SP   DO

1. The timid <u>man</u> <u><u>sipped</u></u> the hot broth.

2. His plastic flute made a distinct tune.

3. The class constructed a huge rocket for the contest.

4. The invention used a hundred magnets.

5. The intense inventor examined her complex plans.

Exercise 5 · Phrase It

▸ Use the penciling strategy to "scoop" the phrases in each sentence.

▸ Read as you would speak them.

▸ The first two are done for you.

1. Inventors have quick minds.

2. They think about problems.

3. Inventors begin with a problem.

4. Cars use too much gas.

5. The gas makes fumes.

6. Make a car of plastic.

7. It would use less gas.

8. Plastic lasts a long time.

9. Less plastic would go into landfills.

10. We would help save our planet.

Unit 13 · Lesson 6

Exercise 6 · Use the Clues

▸ Read each pair of sentences.

▸ Find the pronoun that is circled.

▸ Underline the noun that the pronoun replaces.

▸ Draw an arrow to show the link between the pronoun and the noun it replaced.

1. Inventors have quick minds. (They) think about problems.

2. Inventions impact our lives. (They) make our lives better.

3. A patent confirms your ownership. (It) means that your invention belongs to you.

4. Inventors begin with a problem. They think about (it.)

5. Inventors begin with a problem. This is how (they) think.

Exercise 7 · Rewrite It

▶ Read each sentence pair in Exercise 6, **Use the Clues**.

▶ Replace the circled pronoun with the noun that it represents.

▶ Rewrite the sentence using the noun.

▶ Check for sentence signals—capital letters and end punctuation.

▶ Read the new sentence.

1. _____

2. _____

3. _____

4. _____

5. _____

Exercise 1 · Listening for Stressed Syllables

▸ Listen to each word and sentence your teacher says.

▸ Repeat the word.

▸ Listen for the stressed, or accented, syllable.

▸ Put an X in the box to mark the position of the stressed syllable.

1. ☐☐

2. ☐☐

3. ☐☐

4. ☐☐

5. ☐☐

6. ☐☐

7. ☐☐

8. ☐☐

9. ☐☐

10. ☐☐

Exercise 2 · Contract It

▶ Read each sentence.

▶ Circle the contraction.

▶ Write the contraction and the two words that make up the contracted form.

▶ The first one is done for you.

1. (I'm) about to disrupt the suspect.

2. It's too small and sluggish.

3. He's investing his money in nonfat dressings.

4. It's been uncommon to get tickets on campus.

5. She's ticketing him for littering in the park.

1. I'm = I + am

2. _____

3. _____

4. _____

5. _____

Unit 13 · Lesson 7

Exercise 3 · Choose It and Use It

▸ Fill in the blank with **its** or **it's**.
  Hint: It's = it is.

▸ Substitute **it's** with **it is**.

▸ Reread the sentence to see if it makes sense.

1. Step back in time. _____ 1985.

2. This bike is not ridden. _____ driven.

3. C5 is _____ name.

4. _____ not as big as a ship.

5. Fabric stretches across _____ frame.

6. _____ downside is speed.

7. _____ not fast because _____ engine is run by batteries.

8. You will find that _____ too small and sluggish to drive in traffic.

9. _____ driver is exposed to toxic fumes.

10. _____ an "off-the-wall" invention.

Exercise 4 · Match It: Using Prefixes

▶ Use what you know about the prefix **in-** to match the word to its definition.

▶ Draw a line to match each word to the definition.

▶ Use a dictionary to verify answers.

Word	Definition
1. inland	**a.** to write inside of a book or on a stone
2. income	**b.** into
3. indent	**c.** to notch into an edge
4. inscribe	**d.** located inside of a country, away from the ocean or shore.
5. in-	**e.** money that comes in because of work

▶ Look at definitions for items 1–5. What words to they have in common?

In- means: _____.

▶ Use what you know about the prefix **dis-** to match the word to its definition.

▶ Draw a line to match each word to the definition.

▶ Use a dictionary to verify answers.

Word	Definition
6. disprove	**a.** not to like, the opposite of like.
7. disband	**b.** to move something away from its usual place, often by force
8. dislike	**c.** to prove wrong; to prove that something is the opposite of truth
9. displace	**d.** to break up or undo an organization or group (band)
10. dis-	**e.** apart, away and sometimes the opposite of

▶ Look at definitions for items 6–10. What words to they have in common?

Dis- means: _____.

Exercise 5 · Code It: Noun or Verb

▸ Read each sentence.

▸ Write **N** if the underlined word is a noun. Write **V** if it is a verb.

▸ The first one is done for you.

N

1. <u>Conduct</u> is an aspect of your grade.

2. You <u>conduct</u> the contest by the rules.

3. The <u>object</u> of their plan was escape.

4. I <u>object</u> to the complex plans.

5. Dr. Smith will <u>present</u> the contest rules to the class.

6. His <u>present</u> was an atlas.

7. Will they <u>subject</u> us to a written test?

8. The <u>subject</u> of the test is math.

9. His <u>affect</u> was quite odd.

10. His timid manner will <u>affect</u> us.

Exercise 6 · Use the Clues

▸ Read the passage.

▸ Reread the underlined sentences with circled pronouns.

▸ Draw an arrow to show the link between the circled pronoun and the noun it replaced in the paragraph.

▸ The first one is done for you.

based on "Solving Problems"

Inventors begin with a problem. Cars use too much gas. Make a car of plastic. That could solve it. The car wouldn't be so heavy. It would use less gas. It would pollute less. Plastic lasts a long time. It doesn't rust. The color doesn't fade. There would be a bonus, too. Think of all the juice we drink. Juice comes in plastic jugs. We could reuse them.

Unit 13 · Lesson 7

Exercise 7 · Rewrite It

▸ Reread the underlined sentences in Exercise 6, **Use the Clues**.

▸ Replace the circled pronoun with the noun it represents.

▸ Rewrite the underlined sentences using the nouns.

▸ Check for sentence signals—capital letters and end punctuation.

▸ The first one is done for you.

▸ Share and compare your sentences with a partner.

1. That could solve the problem.

2. _____

3. _____

4. _____

5. _____

Exercise 1 · Listening for Stressed Syllables

▶ Listen to the word your teacher says. Repeat the word.

▶ Listen for the stressed, or accented, syllable.

▶ Write the stressed syllable in the correct box.

	1st Syllable	2nd Syllable
1.		
2.		
3.		
4.		
5.		
6.		
7.		
8.		
9.		
10.		

Unit 13 · Lesson 8

Exercise 2 · Diagram It: Subject, Predicate, and Direct Object

▸ Read each sentence.

▸ Diagram each sentence in the space below.

▸ Do the first two sentences with your teacher.

1. The wind gusted.

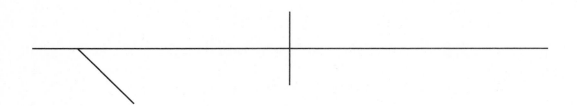

2. The wind affected the crops.

3. Children collected things.

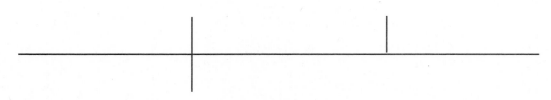

(continued)

Exercise 2 (continued) · Diagram It: Subject, Predicate, and Direct Object

4. Lemons love sun.

5. The code vanished.

Exercise 3 · Use the Clues

▸ Use context clues to define **dirigible**.

- Underline the vocabulary word.

- Read text surrounding the unknown word.

- Underline the words and meaning signals that help define the unknown word.

- Identify and circle the pronoun that refers to the target word.

- Draw an arrow to show the link between the pronoun and the noun it refers to.

- Put a box around a synonym for **dirigible**.

---

from "Way to Go!"

Now That's a Big Balloon!

Can you imagine a dirigible that can carry big loads of cargo and passengers? A dirigible is sometimes called an airship. Actually, it's a huge helium balloon. Propellers move it. It's similar to a blimp. You've seen blimps on TV. They carry television crews over sports fields. There is a difference between a dirigible and a blimp. A dirigible has a rigid inside frame. This means it can be much bigger than a blimp.

▸ Write a definition based on the context clues.

▸ Use a complete sentence.

▸ Verify your definition with the dictionary or www.yourdictionary.com.

   dirigible— _____

_____

▸ Complete the following sentence:

   A synonym for dirigible is _____.

Exercise 4 · Answer It

▸ Underline the signal word in each question.

▸ Write the answers in complete sentences.

▸ Check for sentence signals—capital letters and end punctuation.

1. Plastic like that in juice containers can be used to produce cars. Generalize what other types of containers could provide plastic for the same purpose.

   _____

   _____

   _____

2. Different types of gas have been used to fill dirigibles. What can be inferred about the safety of helium as opposed to hydrogen?

   _____

   _____

   _____

3. Explain why a person does not need a pilot's license to operate a ground-effect plane.

   _____

   _____

   _____

4. Michael Whiting invented a wheelchair that can be used in mountain-trail racing. Generalize other off-road settings where this wheelchair could be used.

   _____

   _____

   _____

Exercise 1 · Listening for Stressed Syllables

▸ Listen to each word and sentence your teacher says.

▸ Repeat the word.

▸ Listen for the stressed, or accented, syllable.

▸ Put an X in the box to mark the position of the stressed syllable.

1. ☐☐   6. ☐☐

2. ☐☐   7. ☐☐

3. ☐☐   8. ☐☐

4. ☐☐   9. ☐☐

5. ☐☐   10. ☐☐

Exercise 2 · Build It

▸ Combine prefixes in the middle square with word parts to form new words.

▸ **Example: un + plug = unplug**.

▸ Record new words in the chart below, according to their prefix.

▸ Use a dictionary to verify that you are building real words.

plug	stick	scribe
connected	in- dis- non- un-	used
-sect	stop	like

non-	un-	in-	dis-

Unit 13 · Lesson 9

▸ Read the passage.

▸ Find and underline (or highlight) compound words.

▸ Find and underline words with these prefixes: **un-**, **in-**, **dis-**, **non-**.

---

based on "Way to Go!"

Now That's a Big Balloon!

A dirigible is sometimes called an airship. Actually, it's a huge helium balloon. It is solar-powered and lighter-than-air. Propellers move it nonstop, long distance through the air. It's similar to the unusual blimps you've seen on TV. They carry television crews over sports fields. There is a difference between a dirigible and a blimp. Unlike a blimp, a dirigible has a rigid inside frame. This means it can be much bigger than a blimp. The best-known dirigible was the *Hindenburg*.

Exercise 4 · Sort It: Compound Words and Words With Prefixes

▶ Sort the underlined words from Exercise 3, **Find It**, into the correct columns.

Compound Words	Words with Prefixes

Exercise 5 · Define It

▶ Circle each word below in "**Now That's a Big Balloon**!" in Exercise 3.

▶ Use context clues and your knowledge of word parts to define the words.

▶ Write the definitions on the lines.

1. <u>solar-powered</u>—

2. <u>nonstop</u>—

3. <u>unlike</u>—

4. <u>inside</u>—

5. <u>best-known</u>—

Unit 13 · Lesson 9

Exercise 6 · Answer It

▸ Use the selection "**Way to Go!**" in the *Student Text*.

▸ Underline the signal word in item 5.

▸ Use the chart below to complete item 5.

5. Working with a partner, sort the meanings of the phrase "way to go" into the following categories: <u>Literal meaning of "way to go"</u> (*a way or direction to travel*) or <u>Figurative meaning of "way to go"</u> (*Good job!*). Write an X under the column you select for each text section.

Text Section	Literal meaning of "way to go"	Figurative meaning of "way to go"
Drink Juice and Drive		
The Ultimate Bike		
Now That's a Big Balloon!		
Skimming the Water		
Now for Something Really Fast		
Wheeling Down the Mountain		

Exercise 7 · Write It: Conclusion Sentence

▸ Read the topic sentence for "**Way to Go!**" with your teacher.

▸ Work with your teacher to list words or phrases that could replace the boxed words.

| Many | inventors have | built | incredible | machines for transportation. |

_____   _____   _____   _____

_____   _____   _____   _____

_____   _____   _____   _____

▸ Choose words to fill in the blanks to create a **paraphrased** sentence.

Reminder: To **paraphrase,** you need to replace words from the text with *your own words*.

_____ inventors have _____ _____ _____ for transportation.
   Many   built   incredible   machines

▸ Write the new sentence below.

▸ Check for sentence signals—capital letters and end punctuation.

_____

_____

Exercise 1 · Listening for Stressed Syllables

▸ Listen to each word your teacher says.

▸ Repeat the word and count the syllables. Write the number in the first column.

▸ Write the letter for the vowel sound you hear in each syllable.

▸ Say the word again. Listen for the stressed syllable.

▸ Circle the vowel in the stressed syllable.

	How many syllables do you hear?	First vowel sound	Second vowel sound
1.			
2.			
3.			
4.			
5.			

Exercise 2 · Sort It: Inventions

▸ Reread the text **"It'll Never Work."**

▸ Locate inventions in the text.

▸ Record each invention in the correct column.

▸ Verify answers with a partner.

▸ The first two are done for you.

vehicles or machines	devices or contraptions
Sinclair C5	spaghetti stretcher

Unit 13 · Lesson 10

Exercise 3 · Listening for Details

▶ Listen to your teacher read **"Way to Go!"**

▶ Write at least one detail about each of the inventions listed in the chart.

▶ Work with a group to add details to your lists.

plastic car	ultimate bike
dirigible	**ground-effect plane**

(continued)

Exercise 3 (continued) · Listening for Details

rocket-on-wheels	off-road wheelchair

Unit 13 · Lesson 10

Exercise 4 · Blueprint for Writing: Developing Main Ideas

▸ Read the topic sentence.

▸ Review the details provided in each section of the outline.

▸ Identify the main idea by considering how the details relate to each other.

▸ Write the main idea for each section of the outline.

▸ Copy your conclusion sentence from Lesson 9, Exercise 7: **Write It: Conclusion Sentence**, to the bottom of the outline.

Many inventors have built incredible machines for transportation. _____

I. _____

    A. Made of plastic _____

    B. Would get 70 miles to the gallon _____

    C. Produces less exhaust _____

    D. Never rusts or needs painting _____

II. _____

    A. Made of carbon-fiber materials _____

    B. Uses a solid wheel _____

    C. Tires made of silk and fiber _____

    D. Light and fast _____

III. _____

    A. A huge helium balloon _____

    B. Propellers move it _____

    C. Has a rigid inside frame _____

    D. Can be much bigger than a blimp _____

(continued)

Exercise 4 *(continued)* · **Blueprint for Writing: Developing Main Ideas**

IV. _____

    A. Flies 3–6 feet above the water _____

    B. Much faster than boats _____

    C. Uses half as much fuel as a plane _____

    D. _____

V. _____

    A. 1–2 jet engines on wheels _____

    B. Can go 700 miles per hour _____

    C. Engines are same as military fighter jets _____

    D. Can be very dangerous _____

VI. _____

    A. Uses best bike technology _____

    B. Moves along wilderness trails _____

    C. Can race down mountains _____

    D. Can go 50 miles per hour _____

_____

Check off the activities you complete with each lesson. Evaluate your accomplishments at the end of each lesson. Pay attention to teacher evaluations and comments.

Unit Objectives	Lesson 1 (Date:_____)	Lesson 2 (Date:_____)
STEP 1 **Phonemic Awareness and Phonics** • Say sounds for vowels <u>ar</u>, <u>or</u>, <u>er</u>, <u>ir</u>, <u>ur</u>. • Write the letters for sounds / âr /, / ôr /, / êr /. • Identify <u>r</u>-controlled syllables. • Identify stressed syllables.	❑ Introduction: r-Controlled Syllables ❑ Vowel Chart (T) ❑ Syllable Awareness: Segmentation	❑ Syllable Awareness: Segmentation ❑ Exercise 1: Listening for Sounds in Words
STEP 2 **Word Recognition and Spelling** • Read and spell words with <u>r</u>-controlled syllables. • Spell / ŭ / with <u>o</u> + <u>er</u> (e.g., other). • Spell words with prefixes: inter-, under-. • Read and spell contractions with are. • Read and spell the **Essential Words**: day, little, may, new, say, may.	❑ Exercise 1: Spelling Pretest 1 ❑ Memorize It	❑ Exercise 2: Sort It: Closed and r-Controlled Syllables ❑ Word Fluency 1 ❑ Memorize It ❑ Handwriting Practice
STEP 3 **Vocabulary and Morphology** • Identify antonyms, synonyms, word attributes, and homophones. • Use the meaning of prefixes to define words. • Use comparative and superlative adjectives.	❑ Unit Vocabulary ❑ K-W-L Organizer (T) ❑ Expression of the Day	❑ Introduction: Degrees of Adjectives ❑ Exercise 3: Rewrite It: Comparative Adjectives ❑ Expression of the Day
STEP 4 **Grammar and Usage** • Identify and use nouns, verbs, and adjectives. • Identify prepositions and prepositional phrases. • Identify the complete subject and predicate. • Identify and write sentences with a compound subject or predicate. • Use the conjunction or to build sentences with compound parts.	❑ Exercise 2: Identify It: Singular and Plural Nouns ❑ Exercise 3: Sort It: Adjectives	❑ Exercise 4: Identify It: Noun, Verb, or Adjective ❑ Exercise 5: Find It and Identify It: Prepositions
STEP 5 **Listening and Reading Comprehension** • Use context-based strategies to define words. • Identify signal words: show, use. • Identify transition words in informational text.	❑ Exercise 4: Phrase It ❑ Independent Text: "Making Art" ❑ Exercise 5: Find It: r-Controlled Syllables	❑ Exercise 6: Use the Clues ❑ Passage Fluency 1
STEP 6 **Speaking and Writing** • Organize main ideas and details for writing. • Write responses to **Answer It** questions with the signal words: show, use. • Use transition words for time sequence in paragraph development.	❑ Masterpiece Sentences: Stages 1 and 2 ❑ Sentence Types: Fact or Opinion?	❑ Exercise 7: Rewrite It: Pronouns
Self-Evaluation (5 is the highest) **Effort** = I produced my best work. **Participation** = I was actively involved in tasks. **Independence** = I worked on my own.	**Effort:** 1 2 3 4 5 **Participation:** 1 2 3 4 5 **Independence:** 1 2 3 4 5	**Effort:** 1 2 3 4 5 **Participation:** 1 2 3 4 5 **Independence:** 1 2 3 4 5
Teacher Evaluation	**Effort:** 1 2 3 4 5 **Participation:** 1 2 3 4 5 **Independence:** 1 2 3 4 5	**Effort:** 1 2 3 4 5 **Participation:** 1 2 3 4 5 **Independence:** 1 2 3 4 5

Lesson 3 (Date:_____)	Lesson 4 (Date:_____)	Lesson 5 (Date:_____)
❑ Syllable Awareness: Segmentation ❑ Exercise 1: Listening for Sounds in Words	❑ Exercise 1: Syllable Awareness: Segmentation	❑ Content Mastery: Syllable Awareness
❑ r-Controlled Syllables ❑ Exercise 2: Sort It: r-Controlled Syllables ❑ Double It (T) ❑ Exercise 3: Find It: Essential Words ❑ Word Fluency 1	❑ Vowel Sounds and Spellings ❑ Exercise 2: Sort It: Sounds for o ❑ Divide It ❑ Double It (T) ❑ Word Fluency 2 ❑ Type It	❑ Content Mastery: Spelling Posttest 1
❑ Exercise 4: Define It ❑ Draw It: Idioms ❑ Expression of the Day	❑ Exercise 3: Rewrite It: Superlative Adjectives ❑ Expression of the Day	❑ Introduction: Reading Word Pairs ❑ Exercise 1: Word Networks: Antonyms, Synonyms, and Attributes ❑ Draw It: Idioms ❑ Expression of the Day
❑ Exercise 5: Identify It: Prepositional Phrases	❑ Exercise 4: Identify It: Forms of Be ❑ Exercise 5: Sort It: Past, Present, and Future Verbs	❑ Introduction: Complete Subject and Complete Predicate ❑ Exercise 2: Identify It: Complete Subject and Complete Predicate ❑ Masterpiece Sentences: Stage 4: Paint Your Subject ❑ Masterpiece Sentences: Using Adjectives
❑ Instructional Text: "From Rock Art to Graffiti" ❑ Exercise 6: Use the Clues	❑ Exercise 6: Blueprint for Reading: Transition Words for Time Sequence (T)	❑ Exercise 6: Blueprint for Reading: Identifying the Details (T) (Lesson 4)
❑ Exercise 7: Answer It	❑ Write It: Topic Sentence ❑ Exercise 7: Blueprint for Writing: Outline (T) ❑ Challenge Text: "Leonardo the Artist"	❑ Exercise 7: Blueprint for Writing: Outline (T) (Lesson 4) ❑ Write It: Time Sequence Paragraph (T) ❑ Challenge Text: "Leonardo the Artist"
Effort: 1 2 3 4 5 Participation: 1 2 3 4 5 Independence: 1 2 3 4 5	Effort: 1 2 3 4 5 Participation: 1 2 3 4 5 Independence: 1 2 3 4 5	Effort: 1 2 3 4 5 Participation: 1 2 3 4 5 Independence: 1 2 3 4 5
Effort: 1 2 3 4 5 Participation: 1 2 3 4 5 Independence: 1 2 3 4 5	Effort: 1 2 3 4 5 Participation: 1 2 3 4 5 Independence: 1 2 3 4 5	Effort: 1 2 3 4 5 Participation: 1 2 3 4 5 Independence: 1 2 3 4 5

Check off the activities you complete with each lesson. Evaluate your accomplishments at the end of each lesson. Pay attention to teacher evaluations and comments.

Unit Objectives	Lesson 6 (Date:_____)	Lesson 7 (Date:_____)
STEP 1 **Phonemic Awareness and Phonics** • Say sounds for vowels <u>ar</u>, <u>or</u>, <u>er</u>, <u>ir</u>, <u>ur</u>. • Write the letters for sounds / âr /, / ôr /, / êr /. • Identify <u>r</u>-controlled syllables. • Identify stressed syllables.	❏ Exercise 1: Listening for Stressed Syllables	❏ Exercise 1: Listening for Stressed Syllables
STEP 2 **Word Recognition and Spelling** • Read and spell words with <u>r</u>-controlled syllables. • Spell / ŭ / with <u>o</u> + <u>er</u> (e.g., other). • Read and spell words with prefixes: inter-, under-. • Read and spell contractions with **are**. • Read and spell the unit **Essential Words**.	❏ Exercise 2: Spelling Pretest 2 ❏ Word Fluency 3	❏ Multisyllable Words ❏ Exercise 2: Build It, Bank It ❏ Exercise 3: Find It: Contractions
STEP 3 **Vocabulary and Morphology** • Identify antonyms, synonyms, word attributes, and homophones. • Use the meaning of prefixes to define words. • Use comparative and superlative adjectives.	❏ Unit Vocabulary ❏ Exercise 3: Word Networks: Antonyms, Synonyms, and Attributes ❏ Expression of the Day	❏ Introduction: Prefixes **inter-** and **under-** ❏ Exercise 4: Define It: Prefixes ❏ Expression of the Day
STEP 4 **Grammar and Usage** • Identify and use nouns, verbs, and adjectives. • Identify prepositions and prepositional phrases. • Identify the complete subject and predicate. • Identify and write sentences with a compound subject or predicate. • Use the conjunction **or** to build sentences with compound parts.	❏ Exercise 4: Combine It: Compound Subjects ❏ Exercise 5: Combine It: Compound Predicates	❏ Exercise 5: Diagram It: Compound Subjects (T)
STEP 5 **Listening and Reading Comprehension** • Use context-based strategies to define words. • Identify signal words: **show**, **use**. • Identify transition words in informational text.	❏ Exercise 6: Phrase It ❏ Independent Text: "Art at Home and Art in Caves" ❏ Exercise 7: Use the Clues	❏ Passage Fluency 2 ❏ Exercise 6: Use the Clues
STEP 6 **Speaking and Writing** • Organize main ideas and details for writing. • Write responses to **Answer It** questions with the signal words: **show**, **use**. • Use transition words for time sequence in paragraph development.	❏ Exercise 8: Rewrite It: Using Synonyms	❏ Exercise 7: Rewrite It: Pronouns
Self-Evaluation (5 is the highest) **Effort** = I produced my best work. **Participation** = I was actively involved in tasks. **Independence** = I worked on my own.	**Effort:** 1 2 3 4 5 **Participation:** 1 2 3 4 5 **Independence:** 1 2 3 4 5	**Effort:** 1 2 3 4 5 **Participation:** 1 2 3 4 5 **Independence:** 1 2 3 4 5
Teacher Evaluation	**Effort:** 1 2 3 4 5 **Participation:** 1 2 3 4 5 **Independence:** 1 2 3 4 5	**Effort:** 1 2 3 4 5 **Participation:** 1 2 3 4 5 **Independence:** 1 2 3 4 5

Lesson 8 (Date:_____)	Lesson 9 (Date:_____)	Lesson 10 (Date:_____)
❑ Exercise 1: Listening for Word Parts	❑ Exercise 1: Listening for Stressed Syllables	❑ Exercise 1: Syllable Awareness: Segmentation
❑ Divide It ❑ Exercise 2: Sort It: Final Sounds ❑ Word Fluency 4	❑ Exercise 2: Build It	❑ Content Mastery: Spelling Posttest 2
❑ Content Mastery: Vocabulary ❑ Content Mastery: Morphology	❑ Exercise 3: Find It: Prefixes ❑ Exercise 4: Sort It: Prefixes ❑ Exercise 5: Use the Clues ❑ Expression of the Day	❑ Exercise 2: Match It: Homophones ❑ Draw It: Idioms ❑ Expression of the Day
❑ Exercise 3: Diagram It: Compound Predicate (T)	❑ Exercise 6: Revise It: Compound Subjects and Compound Predicates	❑ Content Mastery: Parts of Speech ❑ Content Mastery: Complete Subjects and Predicates ❑ Content Mastery: Compound Subjects and Predicates
❑ Instructional Text: "Becoming an Artist" ❑ Exercise 4: Use the Clues	❑ Exercise 7: Answer It	❑ K-W-L Organizer (T)
❑ Exercise 5: Answer It	❑ Write It: Topic Sentence ❑ Exercise 8: Write It: Conclusion Sentence ❑ Challenge Text: "Art in Space"	❑ Exercise 3: Blueprint for Writing: Developing Main Ideas ❑ Challenge Text: "Art in Space"
Effort: 1 2 3 4 5 **Participation:** 1 2 3 4 5 **Independence:** 1 2 3 4 5	**Effort:** 1 2 3 4 5 **Participation:** 1 2 3 4 5 **Independence:** 1 2 3 4 5	**Effort:** 1 2 3 4 5 **Participation:** 1 2 3 4 5 **Independence:** 1 2 3 4 5
Effort: 1 2 3 4 5 **Participation:** 1 2 3 4 5 **Independence:** 1 2 3 4 5	**Effort:** 1 2 3 4 5 **Participation:** 1 2 3 4 5 **Independence:** 1 2 3 4 5	**Effort:** 1 2 3 4 5 **Participation:** 1 2 3 4 5 **Independence:** 1 2 3 4 5

Exercise 1 · Spelling Pretest 1

▶ Write the words your teacher says.

1. _____ 6. _____ 11. _____

2. _____ 7. _____ 12. _____

3. _____ 8. _____ 13. _____

4. _____ 9. _____ 14. _____

5. _____ 10. _____ 15. _____

Exercise 2 · Identify It: Singular and Plural Nouns

▶ Read each sentence.

▶ Decide if the underlined word is singular, plural, or neither.

▶ Put an X in the column to mark your answer.

	Singular	Plural	Neither
1. Keron loves sketching <u>figures</u>.			
2. If you have a <u>pen</u>, you might sketch.			
3. Lines become <u>shapes</u>.			
4. Your work <u>turns</u> into art!			
5. Where are your <u>notes</u>?			

Exercise 3 · Sort It: Adjectives

▶ Read each sentence. The adjective is underlined.

▶ Decide which question the adjective answers.

▶ Write the adjectives in the correct column.

1. Keron's art led to his love of <u>comic</u> books.

2. Keron made a <u>hundred</u> sketches of *The Hulk*.

3. <u>Many</u> people read comic books.

4. Common scraps make <u>fantastic</u> art.

5. Caps from drinks turned into <u>small</u> <u>baking</u> pans.

6. Elisa's scraps became <u>3-D</u> art in her books.

7. Bits of <u>colored</u> rags make a <u>dozen</u> shapes in the book.

8. Twine made a <u>first-rate</u> bird's nest.

Which One?	What Kind?	How Many?

Exercise 4 · Phrase It

▸ Read each sentence.

▸ Use a pencil to "scoop" the phrases in each sentence.

▸ Read the sentences as you would speak them.

▸ The first two are done for you.

1. Sketching is a basic form of art.

2. You're expressing yourself by making art.

3. The bell rings and class begins.

4. Others begin to take notes.

5. You begin to sketch.

6. Your lines become art.

7. Notes will help you pass the test.

8. It's hard to sketch and take notes.

9. Keron began sketching figures.

10. Keron's sketches led him to success.

Exercise 5 · Find It: r-Controlled Syllables

▸ Highlight or underline words with **r**-controlled syllables.

▸ Sort the **r**-controlled syllables according to their spelling.

▸ Write the words under the correct sound.

▸ Record each word once.

---

from "Making Art"

What do you do when you're bored? Some of us just sit and think. Others pick up a pen. If you have a pen, you might sketch. It feels natural. Everybody does it. Sketching is a basic form of art. Lines become shapes. Some shapes are abstract. Even you may not know what they are. Other shapes are concrete. Some of your shapes may turn into objects. Your pad gets filled with art. When you sketch, you're getting absorbed in art. You're expressing yourself by making art.

---

ar	or	ir	er	ur

Exercise 1 · Listening for Sounds in Words

▸ Listen to the word your teacher says.

▸ Identify the **r**-controlled vowel sound.

▸ Mark the **vowel** before the **r** with a circumflex (^).

1. ar   er   or
2. ar   er   or
3. ar   er   or
4. ar   er   or
5. ar   er   or
6. ar   er   or
7. ar   er   or
8. ar   er   or
9. ar   er   or
10. ar   er   or
11. ar   er   or
12. ar   er   or
13. ar   er   or
14. ar   er   or
15. ar   er   or

Exercise 2 · Sort It: Closed and r-Controlled Syllables

▸ Read each word in the **Word Bank**.

▸ Sort each word according to its syllable type.

▸ Write the words under the correct heading.

Word Bank

pat	hut	part	port	bird
bid	chart	north	for	hurt
art	her	mark	chat	pot
girl	star	turn	short	form

Closed Syllable	r-Controlled Syllables		
short vowels	/ âr /	/ ôr /	/ êr /

Exercise 3 · Rewrite It: Comparative Adjectives

▸ Read each adjective.

▸ Add **-er** to make the comparative form of each adjective.

    1. sick   _____

    2. dark   _____

    3. short   _____

    4. fast   _____

    5. smart   _____

▸ Read the comparative adjectives from above.

▸ Choose and write the correct comparative adjectives from above to complete the activities below.

    1. Complete this sentence.

        The kitchen is _____ than the living room, because it has only one window.

    2. Finish the antonym pair.

        taller: _____

    3. Finish the synonym pair:

        quicker: _____

    4. Write a sentence using a comparative adjective.

        _____

    5. Write a word that rhymes.

        quicker: _____

Exercise 4 · Identify It: Noun, Verb, or Adjective

▸ Read these examples with your teacher.

	noun	verb	adjective
Examples: The <u>storm</u> has passed the market.	◯	◯	◯
Do not <u>storm</u> through the market.	◯	◯	◯
The <u>storm</u> door is broken.	◯	◯	◯

▸ Read each sentence.

▸ Look at the underlined word in each sentence.

▸ Use the context to decide if the underlined word is a noun, verb, or adjective.

▸ Fill in the correct bubble.

	noun	verb	adjective
1. He sketched *The Hulk* on <u>chart</u> paper.	◯	◯	◯
2. The <u>comic</u> is on stage.	◯	◯	◯
3. Keron's figures are in <u>comic</u> books.	◯	◯	◯
4. <u>Mexican</u> murals had a purpose.	◯	◯	◯
5. They <u>painted</u> murals on walls.	◯	◯	◯
6. The <u>painted</u> murals were shared with others.	◯	◯	◯
7. The artist made a <u>sketch</u> inside the cave.	◯	◯	◯
8. They will <u>sketch</u> pictures that tell tales.	◯	◯	◯

(continued)

Unit 14 · Lesson 2

Exercise 4 (continued) · Identify It: Noun, Verb, or Adjective

	noun	verb	adjective
9. <u>Rock</u> is cut or carved with messages.	◯	◯	◯
10. <u>Rock</u> art reflects the times when it was made.	◯	◯	◯

Exercise 5 · Find It and Identify It: Prepositions

▸ Read the short passages.

▸ Highlight the prepositions.

▸ Identify whether the prepositions show position in space, time, or neither.

▸ Record the prepositions in the correct column.

> **based on "Becoming an Artist" and "From Rock Art to Graffiti"**
>
> Keron Grant was born in Jamaica in 1976. As a kid, he liked sketching and comics. At 14, he came to the USA. He began sketching figures. Keron's sketches led him to success.
>
> Keith Haring was from New York. In 1980, Haring began drawing graffiti on the streets. He invented his own tag, or signature. He left his tag near each drawing in the subway.

Positions in Space	Positions in Time	Neither

Exercise 6 · Use the Clues

▸ Read each sentence pair.

▸ Read the pronoun that is circled.

▸ Underline the noun that the pronoun is replacing.

▸ Draw an arrow to link the pronoun to the noun it replaced.

1. Meet Keron Grant. (He) was born in Jamaica in 1976.

2. Keron loved *The Hulk*. As a kid, Keron liked sketching (him).

3. The 14-year-old boy came to the United States. (He) visited a comic book store.

4. Keron's figures are in comic books. *Iron Man* was one of (his) creations.

5. Keron began sketching figures. Today, (his) figures are in comic books.

Exercise 7 · Rewrite It: Pronouns

▸ Reread each pair of sentences in Exercise 6, **Use the Clues**.

▸ Replace the pronoun with the noun that it represents.

▸ Rewrite the sentence using the noun.

▸ Check for sentence signals—capital letters, commas, and end punctuation.

▸ Read the new sentence.

▸ Do the first one with your teacher.

1. _____

2. _____

3. _____

4. _____

5. _____

Exercise 1 · Listening for Sounds in Words

▸ Listen to each word your teacher says.

▸ Write the letter or letters where you hear the designated sound.

1. ☐☐☐☐

2. ☐☐☐☐

3. ☐☐☐☐

4. ☐☐☐

5. ☐☐☐

6. ☐☐☐

7. ☐☐☐

8. ☐☐☐

9. ☐☐☐☐☐

10. ☐☐☐☐

Exercise 2 · Sort It: r-Controlled Syllables

▸ Read the words in the **Word Bank**.

▸ Sort the words with **r**-controlled syllables according to their vowel sound and spelling.

▸ Write the words under the correct heading.

Word Bank

burn	short	bar	dark	verb
her	bird	fern	first	star
girl	stir	church	corn	hurt

/ êr / = ir	/ êr / = er	/ êr / = ur	/ âr / = ar	/ ôr / = or

Unit 14 · Lesson 3

Exercise 3 · Find It: Essential Words

▸ Find the **Essential Words** for this unit in these sentences.

▸ Underline the words. There may be more than one in a sentence.

▸ See the *Student Text* for the list of **Essential Words**, if needed.

1. The girl is too little to ride a bike.

2. Did you have a hard day at work?

3. May I have the first turn?

4. Does your bird say much?

5. I entered the park a new way.

▸ Write the **Essential Words** in the spaces.

▸ Circle the four **Essential Words** that rhyme.

_____   _____   _____

_____   _____   _____

Exercise 4 · Define It

▸ Fill in the blanks with a category and an attribute to define the word.

▸ If you are unsure of your definition, compare it with a dictionary.

▸ Do the first definition with your teacher.

1. An **artist** is _____ who _____
                    category   **attribute(s)**

   _____

   _____ .

2. A **car** is _____ that _____
                  category   **attribute(s)**

   _____

   _____ .

3. A **porch** is _____ that _____
                  category   **attribute(s)**

   _____

   _____ .

4. **Corn** is _____ that _____
                category   **attribute(s)**

   _____

   _____ .

5. A **desert** is _____ that _____
                  category   **attribute(s)**

   _____

   _____ .

6. A **farm** is _____ that _____
                  category   **attribute(s)**

   _____

   _____ .

(continued)

Exercise 4 (continued) · Define It

7. A **garden** is _____ that _____

                        category   **attribute(s)**

_____

_____.

8. A **horse** is _____ that _____

                        category   **attribute(s)**

_____

_____.

9. A **park** is _____ that _____

                        category   **attribute(s)**

_____

_____.

10. A **river** is _____ that _____

                        category   **attribute(s)**

_____

_____.

▸ Which vocabulary words are related to land?

▸ Write the words in the blanks.

_____   _____   _____

_____

Exercise 5 · Identify It: Prepositional Phrases

▸ Read each sentence.

▸ Reread the prepositional phrase that is underlined in each sentence.

▸ Circle the preposition.

▸ Put an X in the correct column to show if the prepositional phrase shows:

- Position in *space*, or

- Position in *time*.

	Space	Time
1. Just sit and think <u>in the yard</u>.		
2. <u>Before you know it</u>, lines become shapes.		
3. Take notes <u>during class</u>.		
4. Sketch <u>after class</u>.		
5. It's hard to sketch and take notes <u>at the same time</u>.		
6. Your sketch paper is <u>inside the cabinet</u>.		
7. Keron Grant was born <u>in Jamaica</u>.		
8. Keron Grant was born <u>in 1976</u>.		
9. <u>Since his arrival</u> to the USA, he loved comic books.		
10. Since his arrival <u>to the USA</u>, he loved comic books.		

Unit 14 · Lesson 3

Exercise 6 · Use the Clues

▶ Use meaning signals to define **pictographs** and **engravings**.

- Underline the vocabulary words.

- Read the text before and after the unknown words.

- Underline the word or words that help define each unknown word.

- Circle the meaning signal words and draw a line to the vocabulary word.

> **based on "From Rock Art to Graffiti"**
>
> There are different kinds of rock art. Early types are *pictographs*. These are drawings or paintings on rocks. The painter uses fingers or a brush. *Engravings* are forms of rock art. The rock surface is cut. This leaves pictures on the rock.

▶ Write a definition based on the context clues.

▶ Verify your definition with the dictionary or www.yourdictionary.com.

pictographs— _____

engravings— _____

Exercise 7 · Answer It

▸ Underline the signal word in the question.

▸ Write the answer in complete sentences.

▸ Check for sentence signals—capital letters, commas, and end punctuation.

1. There are many types of rock art. What can you infer about the types of tools used to create engravings, petroglyphs, and sculptures?

   _____

   _____

   _____

2. Define muralist in your own words.

   _____

   _____

   _____

3. Using a timeline, show the progression of rock art from prehistoric cave paintings to modern graffiti.

Past		Present

(continued)

4. The text describes the development of rock art throughout history. Predict what rock art will look like in the future.

_____

_____

_____

5. Lines 97 and 98 use the metaphor "the electricity of his work." What does this phrase tell you about Haring's work?

_____

_____

_____

Exercise 1 · Syllable Awareness: Segmentation

▶ Listen to the word your teacher says.

▶ Count the syllables. Write the number of syllables in the first column.

▶ Write the letter or letters for each vowel sound you hear.

▶ Mark short vowels with a breve (˘).

▶ For **r**-controlled vowels, mark the vowel before the **r** with a circumflex (^).

	How many syllables do you hear?	First vowel sound	Second vowel sound	Third vowel sound
1.				
2.				
3.				
4.				
5.				
6.				
7.				
8.				
9.				
10.				

Unit 14 · Lesson 4

Exercise 2 · Sort It: Sounds for o

▸ Read each word in the **Word Bank**.

▸ Sort each word according to the sound represented by the letter **o**.

▸ Write the word in the chart under the correct heading.

Word Bank

born	correct	mother	brother
morning	cover	north	monster
other	shorter	another	modern
optical	wonder	boxcar	core

o = / ŭ / + er	o + r = / ôr /	o = / ŏ /

Exercise 3 · Rewrite It: Superlative Adjectives

▸ Read each adjective.

▸ Add **-est** to make the superlative form of each adjective.

1. sick   _____

2. dark   _____

3. short   _____

4. fast   _____

5. smart   _____

▸ Choose and write the correct superlative adjective from above to complete the activities that follow.

1. Complete the sentence.

She was the _____ of those who had the flu.

2. Finish the antonym pair.

tallest: _____

3. Finish the synonym pair.

quickest: _____

4. Write a sentence.

_____

5. Write the comparative form of the last adjective in the list.

_____

Unit 14 · Lesson 4

Exercise 4 · Identify It: Forms of *Be*

▸ Read each sentence.

▸ Underline the entire verb phrase once and the main verb twice.

▸ The first one is done as an example.

1. It <u>is <u><u>storming</u></u></u> now.

2. They are scoring the reports for us.

3. He was exploring these segments.

4. We will be ordering the ones we like best.

5. We were wondering if your project would be finished in time.

Exercise 5 · Sort It: Past, Present, and Future Verbs

▶ Read the verbs and verb phrases in the **Verb Bank**.

▶ Identify the time conveyed by these words or phrases.

▶ Record each verb or verb phrase under the correct position on the **Tense Timeline**.

▶ The first one is done for you.

Verb Bank

was marking	is coloring	burns
harvested	infers	am hammering
occurred	will permit	were serving
will understand	marketed	will be entering
will chart	are hurting	will be interacting

Yesterday	Today	Tomorrow
Past	Present	Future
1. was marking	1.	1.
2.	2.	2.
3.	3.	3.
4.	4.	4.
5.	5.	5.

Unit 14 · Lesson 4

Exercise 6 · Blueprint for Reading: Transition Words for Time Sequence

▸ Read each titled section of text.

▸ Highlight the main idea of each section in blue.

▸ Circle the transition words in each section.

---

from "From Rock Art to Graffiti"

What Is Rock Art?

From the beginning, humans made rock art. So what is rock art? It's the marks that have been found on rocks. They have been cut or carved. They have been etched or drawn.

There are different kinds of rock art. Pictographs and engravings are types of rock art. Other types of rock art include petroglyphs, sculptures, and reliefs.

Ancient rock art had different purposes. Some rock art recorded events from the past. Some rock art probably told stories.

(continued)

Mexican Murals: Rock Art Finds Walls

During the nineteenth century, artists in Mexico painted murals. They painted them in village churches. They painted them on outside walls. Shops, taverns, and hotels have murals. All over Mexico, walls are covered with beautiful paintings.

Many of the Mexican murals had a purpose. In the early 1900s, several Mexican artists were caught up in their revolution. Their murals celebrated the triumph of the revolution. The murals also showed the rich cultural heritage of Mexico.

Three of Mexico's most famous muralists were Diego Rivera, Jose Clemente Orozco, and David Siqueiros. All were trained artists. During the early 1900s, they renewed Mexico's great mural-making tradition. They used bold colors. They created striking images.

(continued)

American Graffiti Artist: Modern Rock Art

Today, graffiti has become a modern form of rock art. Keith Haring was an art student. He immersed himself in graffiti. Like in many cities, graffiti grew on the walls and in the subways of New York.

Like other graffiti artists, he invented his own tag, or signature. His first tag was an animal. Then, he drew a little person crawling on all fours. Eventually, it became known as "The Baby." Haring's drawings were simple. He drew pyramids and flying saucers. He drew humans and winged figures. He drew television sets, animals, and yes, babies.

Haring started to become famous. People on the subway saw his work. It was on TV. It was in the newspaper. Soon, New Yorkers wanted his work. They wanted it for their living rooms. His first art show was a huge success. More than 4,000 people came.

Exercise 7 · Blueprint for Writing: Outline

▸ Use the highlighted text for Exercise 6, **Blueprint for Reading**, to complete the outline.

▸ Write the main ideas on the lines beginning with Roman numerals.

▸ Add the transition words to the outline by drawing circles in the margins next to the main ideas. Write the transition words inside the circles.

▸ Do the first two sections with your teacher.

I. _____

    A. _____

    B. _____

    C. _____

    D. _____

II. _____

    A. _____

    B. _____

    C. _____

    D. _____

III. _____

    A. _____

    B. _____

    C. _____

    D. _____

Exercise 1 · Word Networks: Antonyms, Synonyms, and Attributes

Antonyms

▶ Read the words in the **Word Bank**.

▶ Choose and write the word from the **Word Bank** that is an antonym (opposite).

▶ Read the word pairs. Discuss your answers.

Word Bank

summer	send	over
after	long	import

1. short: _____

2. under: _____

3. winter: _____

4. export: _____

5. before: _____

Synonyms

▶ Read the words in the **Word Bank**.

▶ Choose and write the word from the **Word Bank** that is a synonym (same or almost the same).

▶ Read the word pairs. Discuss your answers.

Word Bank

spin	after	method
occur	send	rug

Exercise 1 *(continued)* · **Word Networks: Antonyms, Synonyms, and Attributes**

    6. carpet: _____

    7. twirl: _____

    8. export: _____

    9. happen: _____

    10. way: _____

Attributes

▸ Read the words in the **Word Bank**.

▸ Choose and write the word from the **Word Bank** that is an attribute (shows a relationship or association).

▸ Read the word pairs. Discuss your answers.

Word Bank

morning	current	long
plant	harvest	bumper

    11. river: _____

    12. corn: _____

    13. car: _____

    14. garden: _____

    15. day: _____

Unit 14 · Lesson 5

Exercise 2 · Identify It: Complete Subject and Complete Predicate

▸ Read each sentence.

▸ Identify the complete subject. Underline it once.

▸ Identify the complete predicate. Underline it twice.

1. Early humans created rock art.

2. Rock art has changed over time.

3. Mexican artists created murals.

4. These murals were painted on walls.

5. Graffiti artists create a form of rock art.

Exercise 1 · Listening for Stressed Syllables

▸ Listen to the word your teacher says.

▸ Repeat the word.

▸ Listen for the stressed syllable.

▸ Mark an X in the box to mark the position of the stressed syllable.

	1st Syllable	2nd Syllable
Example: sculpture	X	
1. explore		
2. under		
3. summer		
4. wonder		
5. harvest		

Exercise 2 · Spelling Pretest 2

▶ Write the words your teacher says.

1. _____   6. _____   11. _____

2. _____   7. _____   12. _____

3. _____   8. _____   13. _____

4. _____   9. _____   14. _____

5. _____   10. _____   15. _____

Exercise 3 · Word Networks: Antonyms, Synonyms, and Attributes

▸ Read the word pairs.

▸ Sort the word pairs according to their relationship.

▸ Write the word pairs in the appropriate column.

▸ Discuss your answers with a partner.

import: export	export: send	over: under	corn: harvest
river: current	before: after	happen: occur	plant: garden
way: method	day: morning	short: long	winter: summer

Antonyms (opposite)	Synonyms (same)	Attributes (associations)

Unit 14 · Lesson 6

Exercise 4 · Combine It: Compound Subjects

▸ Read each pair of sentences.

▸ Combine the sentences using the conjunction in parentheses.

▸ Write the new sentence.

▸ Circle both subjects in the sentence you write.

1. The doctor will help them. The nurse will help them. (and)

_____

2. Calder made art. Picasso made art. (and)

_____

3. Shops have murals. Hotels have murals. (and)

_____

4. Yarn can make fantastic art. Twine can make fantastic art. (or)

_____

5. Graffiti is rock art. Wall paintings are rock art. (or)

_____

Exercise 5 · Combine It: Compound Predicates

▶ Read each pair of sentences.

▶ Combine these sentences using the conjunction in parentheses.

▶ Write the new sentence.

▶ Circle both predicates in the sentence you write.

1. An artist sculpts stone. An artist carves stone. (or)

_____

2. Calder imagined the mobile. Calder invented the mobile. (and)

_____

3. The cave dwellers hunted. The cave dwellers fished. (and)

_____

4. People etched on cave walls. People drew on cave walls. (or)

_____

5. Water didn't hurt the etchings. Water didn't wash away the etchings. (or)

_____

Exercise 6 · Phrase It

▶ Use the penciling strategy to "scoop" the phrases in each sentence.

▶ Read the sentences as you would speak them.

▶ The first two are done for you.

1. Elisa used scraps to make art.

2. Elisa's scraps became 3-D art.

3. Elisa had discovered something.

4. Common scraps can make fantastic art.

5. The first form of art was cave art.

6. A hundred tales are told in cave art.

7. Cave art tells the tales of cave people.

8. The cave dwellers hunted and fished.

9. They made messages for each other.

10. From cave art, we learn history.

Exercise 7 · Use the Clues

▶ Read the excerpt from **"Art at Home and Art in Caves."**

▶ Read the underlined phrase in each paragraph.

▶ Circle the word or words in the paragraph that are substituted for the underlined phrase.

▶ Record substitutions on the lines below the text.

---

from "Art at Home and Art in Caves"

Where Did Art Start?

The first form of art was cave art. **<u>Cave artists</u>** made lots of sketches inside caves. Cave art tells the tales of the lives of cave people. The cave dwellers hunted and fished. They made messages for each other. The art they made is still there. The messages they left us tell us much. From cave art, we learn history. We learn about the lives of some of the first humans. We learn something even more important. We learn that humans have always been obsessed with making art.

Substitutions for **cave artists**: _____

Unit 14 · Lesson 6

▸ Read the following sentences.

▸ Substitute the underlined word(s) with a synonym or phrase that means the same thing.

▸ Rewrite the sentences.

▸ Check for sentence signals—capital letters and end punctuation.

▸ Read the new sentences.

1. <u>Fame</u> was in store for Elisa Kleven.

_____

2. She began to tell <u>little tales</u>.

_____

3. Common scraps can make <u>fantastic</u> art.

_____

4. Cave artists made a lot of <u>sketches</u> inside caves.

_____

5. They <u>made messages for</u> each other.

_____

Exercise 1 · Listening for Stressed Syllables

▸ Listen to the word your teacher says. Repeat the word.

▸ Listen for the stressed, or accented, syllable.

▸ Put an X in the box to mark the position of the stressed syllable.

1. ☐☐

2. ☐☐

3. ☐☐

4. ☐☐

5. ☐☐

6. ☐☐

7. ☐☐

8. ☐☐

9. ☐☐

10. ☐☐

Exercise 2 · Build It, Bank It

▸ Read the syllables in the box.

▸ Circle the prefixes.

▸ Combine prefixes with base words and roots to make words. Try to make as many words as possible.

▸ Record the words on the lines below.

▸ Check a dictionary to verify that words are real words.

pass	inter	stand	ject
shirt	mit	pret	under
act	brush	hand	est

_____   _____

_____   _____

_____   _____

_____   _____

_____   _____

Exercise 3 · Find It: Contractions

▸ Read the sentences.

▸ Circle the contractions.

▸ Expand the contractions into two words.

1. We're interested in ordering another pattern. _____

2. Perhaps they're covering their artwork with the plastic. _____

3. You're permitted to enter over there. _____

4. We're trying to understand your book order. _____

5. They're interacting very well with the third doctor. _____

Unit 14 · Lesson 7

Exercise 4 · Define It: Prefixes

▸ Use what you know about the prefix **inter-** to match each word to its definition.

▸ Draw a line to match the word to the correct definition.

▸ Use a dictionary to verify the definitions.

Words	Definitions
1. Internet	**a.** to break into a conversation among people
2. interconnected computers	**b.** between or among nations
3. interstellar	**c.** between or among the stars
4. interrupt	**d.** computers networked between or among people
5. international	**e.** a network between and among people

▸ Look at the definitions for items 1–5. What words do the definitions have in common?

Inter- means: _____.

▸ Use what you know about the prefix **under-** to match each word to its definition.

▸ Draw a line to match the word to the correct definition.

▸ Use a dictionary to verify the definitions.

Words	Definitions
1. underbid	**a.** to charge below the price, not to charge enough
2. undercharge	**b.** to shoot below or shorter than the needed distance
3. underarm	**c.** beneath or below
4. undershot	**d.** to offer an amount below others or below cost
5. under	**e.** to throw by swinging the arm below the shoulder

▸ Look at definitions for items 1–5. What words do they have in common?

Under- means: _____.

Exercise 5 · Diagram It: Compound Subjects

▶ Review these areas of the diagram with your teacher:

    1. Subject: Who (what) did it?

    2. Predicate: What did they (he, she, it) do?

    3. Direct Object: What (who) did they do it to?

▶ Read each sentence.

▶ The compound subject is underlined.

▶ Do the first diagram with your teacher.

▶ Diagram the rest of the sentences.

    1. <u>The doctor or the nurse</u> will help.

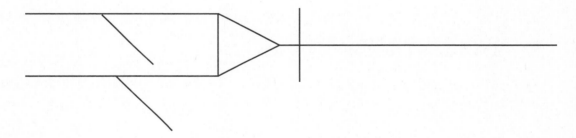

    2. <u>Calder and Picasso</u> made art.

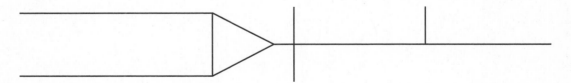

(continued)

Exercise 5 (continued) · Diagram It: Compound Subjects

3. <u>Shops and hotels</u> have murals.

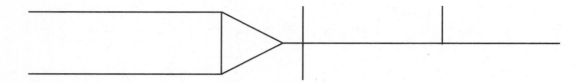

4. <u>Yarn or twine</u> can make fantastic art.

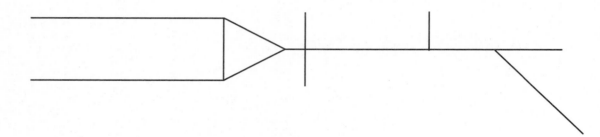

5. <u>Graffiti or wall painting</u> makes rock art.

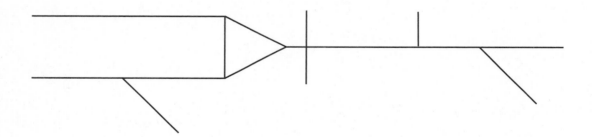

Exercise 6 · Use the Clues

▶ Read the passage.

▶ Reread the underlined sentences.

▶ Draw an arrow from the circled pronouns to the words they represent.

---

from "Art at Home and Art in Caves"

Fame was in store for Elisa Kleven. (She) made a name for herself. It began
when she was a little girl. Common scraps fascinated (her). (She) used scraps
to make art. Nutshells became beds. Caps from drinks became small baking
pans. (She) loved to make little settings. The settings Elisa created inspired her.
(She) began to tell little tales.

Exercise 7 · Rewrite It: Pronouns

▶ Reread the passage in Exercise 6, **Use the Clues**.

▶ Rewrite the underlined sentences replacing the pronoun with a noun that it represents.

▶ Check for sentence signals—capital letters and end punctuation.

▶ Read your sentences to a partner.

1. Elisa Kleven made a name for herself.

2. _____

3. _____

4. _____

5. _____

Exercise 1 · Listening for Word Parts

▸ Listen to each word your teacher says.

▸ Mark whether or not you hear a suffix.

▸ If yes, spell the suffix.

	Do you hear a suffix on the word?		If yes, spell the suffix.
	Yes	No	
1.			
2.			
3.			
4.			
5.			
6.			
7.			
8.			
9.			
10.			

Exercise 2 · Sort It: Final Sounds

▶ Read the words in the **Word Bank**.

▶ Work in small groups or with a partner.

▶ Sort the words according to a spelling or syllable pattern.

▶ Label the headings.

Word Bank

carve	horse	serve	starve
verse	observe	forgive	remorse
have	nurse	give	purse

Unit 14 · Lesson 8

Exercise 3 · Diagram It: Compound Predicate

▶ Review these areas of the diagram with your teacher:

    1. Subject: Who (what) did it?

    2. Predicate: What did they (he, she, it) do?

    3. Direct Object: What (who) did they do it to?

▶ Read each sentence.

▶ The compound predicate is underlined.

▶ Do the first diagram with your teacher.

▶ Diagram the rest of the sentences.

    1. An artist <u>carves or sculpts</u> stone.

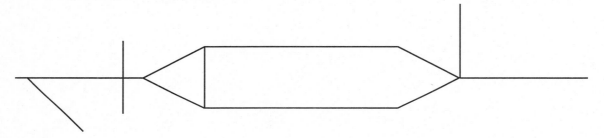

    2. Calder <u>imagined and invented</u> the mobile.

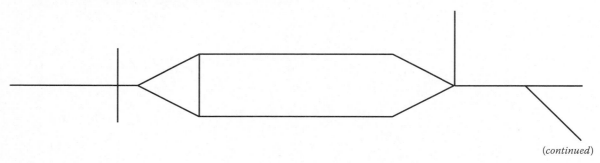

(continued)

Exercise 3 (continued) · **Diagram It: Compound Predicate**

3. The cave dwellers <u>hunted and fished</u>.

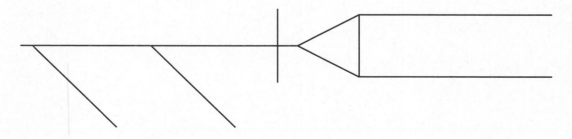

4. People <u>etched or drew</u> marks on cave walls.

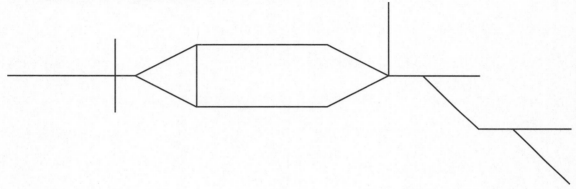

5. Water did not <u>hurt or wash</u> the etchings away.

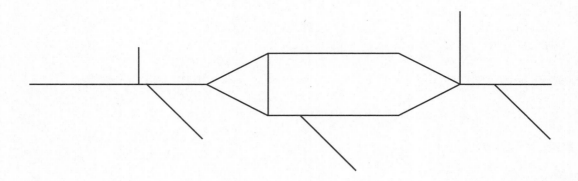

Unit 14 • Lesson 8

Exercise 4 • Use the Clues

▸ Reread the text.

▸ Use context clues and meaning signals to define the word **mobile**.

▸ Underline the vocabulary word.

▸ Read the text before and after the unknown word.

▸ Underline the words that define the unknown word.

---

from "Becoming an Artist"

Calder's art is known for motion. For ideas, he watched machines. "I was always delighted by the cable car. . . . The machinery and movement interested me." He studied to be a mechanical engineer. He wanted to learn to make structures and machines. Calder also imagined moving art. So he invented the mobile—art that swings in the air. His art is playful, and some of his biggest fans are kids. After an exhibit of his work in New York, he joked, "My fan mail is enormous—everyone is under 6."

▸ Write a definition based on the context clues.

▸ Verify your definition with the dictionary or www.yourdictionary.com.

▸ Write a sentence using the word **mobile**.

Define It:

mobile— _____

_____

Sentence:

_____

_____

Exercise 5 · Answer It

▸ Underline the signal word in the question.

▸ Write the answers in complete sentences.

▸ Check for sentence signals—capital letters and end punctuation.

1. What can you generalize about the artists described in this selection from reading the first sentence under each section's heading?

_____

_____

_____

2. Describe the meaning of Augusta Savage's sculpture titled "The Harp."

_____

_____

_____

3. Explain what Alexander Calder meant when he said, "My fan mail is enormous—everyone is under 6."

_____

_____

_____

(continued)

4. Use a Venn diagram to list the similarities and differences between the art of Elisa Kleven and Keron Grant.

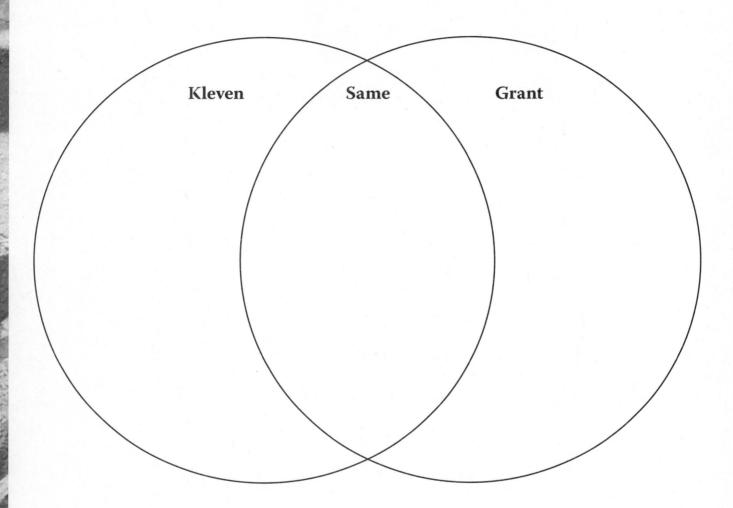

Lesson 9

Exercise 1 · Listening for Stressed Syllables

▸ Listen to each word your teacher says.

▸ Repeat the word.

▸ Listen for the stressed, or accented, syllable.

▸ Put an X in the box to mark the position of the stressed syllable.

1. ☐☐   6. ☐☐

2. ☐☐   7. ☐☐

3. ☐☐   8. ☐☐

4. ☐☐   9. ☐☐

5. ☐☐   10. ☐☐

Exercise 2 · Build It

▸ Combine prefixes in the middle square with base words to form new words.
Example: under- + cover = undercover.

▸ Record words in the chart below according to their prefix.

▸ Use a dictionary to verify that you are building real words.

take	arm	cover
hand	inter- under- un- in- dis-	lace
lay	mix	done

under-	inter-	un-	in-	dis-

Exercise 3 · Find It: Prefixes

▶ Read the section below.

▶ Find and underline the words with these prefixes:
under-, inter-, un-, in-, dis-, non-.

---

based on "Becoming an Artist"

Comic Book Artist at Work

Late one afternoon, a big school bus rumbled down the road. It drove past the intersection and toward the underpass by Keron Grant's home. His cousin pulled out paper and a pencil and started drawing. Keron's 3-year-old eyes were glued to the paper as the form of the bus became distinct. Keron discovered an instant love for drawing. Soon after that, he started drawing his own pictures. Keron had an inborn, uncanny talent for drawing.

Keron entered art school intending to learn to design cars. However, he kept on drawing comics nonstop. Keron was discovered when he began to display his intense comic book characters in public. Keron Grant now creates issues of *Iron Man* for Marvel Comics and he's known internationally. He is known in many countries. All artists show what they feel about the world in their art.

Exercise 4 · Sort It: Prefixes

▸ Sort the words from Exercise 3, **Find It: Prefixes**, by their prefixes.

under-	inter-	un-

in-	non-	dis-

Exercise 5 · Use the Clues

▸ Work with your teacher to define the target words below.

▸ Circle each vocabulary word in the text from Exercise 3: **Find It: Prefixes**.

▸ Use the context and meaning of the prefix and base or root word to define the words.

▸ Write the definitions on the lines below.

intersection—_____

_____

underpass—_____

_____

instant—_____

_____

nonstop—_____

_____

internationally—_____

_____

Unit 14 • Lesson 9

Exercise 6 · Revise It: Compound Subjects and Compound Predicates

▸ Read the text.

▸ Reread the underlined sentences.

▸ Use a conjunction (**and**/**or**) to combine the subjects or predicates.

▸ Write the new sentence on the numbered line in the text below.

▸ Check for sentence signals—capital letters and end punctuation.

▸ Reread the new text together with your teacher.

---

based on "Art at Home" and "Art in Caves"

Elisa used scraps to make art. Yarn can make fantastic art. Twine can make
                                                                    1
fantastic art. Nutshells became 3-D art. Caps became 3-D art. Elisa's scraps
          1   2
became 3-D art in her books.

The first form of art was cave art. Wind didn't hurt cave art. Water didn't
                                                                       3
hurt cave art. Cave art tells tales of the lives of cave people. The cave dwellers
     3   4
hunted. The cave dwellers fished. They sketched crude maps. They made
                    4   5
messages for each other.
          5

Elisa used scraps to make art. _____.
                                                    1
_____. Elisa's scraps became 3-D art
                        2
in her books. The first form of art was cave art. _____
                                                              3
_____. Cave art tells tales of the lives
of cave people. _____.
                                      4
_____
                        5
_____.

Exercise 7 · Answer It

▶ Listen to your teacher read **"Becoming an Artist."**

▶ Work with a partner to answer the question. Focus on each artist and the type of art each created. Do the first artist with your teacher.

5. <u>Sort</u> the five artists listed below into the category that classifies the type of art created by each artist.

Artists: Alexander Calder, Keron Grant, Augusta Savage, Elisa Kleven, Pablo Picasso

Painting/Drawing	Sculpture	Collage

Unit 14 · Lesson 9

Exercise 8 · Write It: Conclusion Sentence

▸ Read the topic sentence for **"Becoming an Artist"** with your teacher.

▸ Work with your teacher to list words or phrases that could replace the boxed words.

▸ Write your ideas below the boxed words to create options for a new topic sentence.

Reminder: To **paraphrase**, you need to replace words from the text with *your own words*.

"Becoming an Artist" topic sentence:

| Numerous | | great | artists began | creating | art as | children | . |

_____   _____   _____   _____

_____   _____   _____   _____

_____   _____   _____   _____

▸ Choose words to fill in the blanks to **paraphrase** the boxed words.

_____ _____ artists
            Numerous   great

began _____ art as _____.
           creating   children

▸ Write the answer here.

▸ Check for sentence signals—capital letters and end punctuation.

_____

_____

Exercise 1 · Syllable Awareness: Segmentation

▸ Listen to each word your teacher says.

▸ Count the syllables. Write the number in the first column.

▸ Write the letter or letters for the vowel sounds you hear in each word.

▸ Say the word again. Listen for the stressed syllable.

▸ Circle the vowel in the stressed syllable.

	How many syllables do you hear?	First vowel sound	Second vowel sound
1.			
2.			
3.			
4.			
5.			

Unit 14 · Lesson 10

Exercise 2 · Match It: Homophones

▸ Read the homophones and the definitions.

▸ Draw a line to match each homophone with its definition.

▸ Use a dictionary, if necessary.

1. there		**a.**	thick coat of hair
2. fir		**b.**	you + are
3. your		**c.**	possessive form of you
4. they're		**d.**	place
5. fur		**e.**	evergreen tree
6. their		**f.**	they + are
7. you're		**g.**	new life
8. birth		**h.**	possessive form of they
9. berth		**i.**	sleeping compartment or bunk

Exercise 3 · Blueprint for Writing: Developing Main Ideas

▸ Read the topic sentence.

▸ Read each set of details provided on the outline.

▸ Identify the main idea for each set of details.

▸ Write the main idea for each section of the outline.

▸ Copy the conclusion sentence from Lesson 9, Exercise 8, **Write It: Conclusion Sentence**, on the bottom of the outline.

Numerous great artists began creating art as children. _____

I. _____

    A. began drawing at a very young age _____

    B. had amazing art talent _____

    C. saw art in new ways _____

    D. _____

II. _____

    A. wanted to be an artist at 17 _____

    B. moved to Harlem _____

    C. made sculptures that reflect African American culture ____

    D. taught art to children and adults _____

(continued)

Exercise 3 (continued) · Blueprint for Writing: Developing Main Ideas

III. _____

    A. began as a child _____

    B. loved machinery and things that moved _____

    C. invented mobiles _____

    D. _____

IV. _____

    A. child artist _____

    B. created a dollhouse for toy creatures _____

    C. draws 3D illustrations for children's books _____

    D. makes collages _____

V. _____

    A. began at age 3 _____

    B. from Jamaica _____

    C. drew comics in grade school _____

    D. still creates *Iron Man* comics _____

_____

_____

Check off the activities you complete with each lesson. Evaluate your accomplishments at the end of each lesson. Pay attention to teacher evaluations and comments.

	Unit Objectives	Lesson 1 (Date:_____)	Lesson 2 (Date:_____)
STEP 1	**Phonemic Awareness and Phonics** • Segment and delete syllables from multisyllable words. • Say long vowel sounds for: <u>a</u>, <u>e</u>, <u>i</u>, <u>o</u>, <u>u</u>. • Identify **open** syllables. • Identify stressed syllables.	❏ Introduction: Open Syllables ❏ Phoneme Production/Replication ❏ Syllable Awareness: Segmentation	❏ Syllable Awareness: Deletion ❏ Vowel Chart ❏ Exercise 1: Listening for Sounds in Words
STEP 2	**Word Recognition and Spelling** • Read and spell words with **open** syllables. • Read and spell the **Essential Words**: *good, great, right, though, through, year*. • Spell words with prefixes: **pre-, re-, super-**. • Read and spell contractions with **have**. • Add **-es** to words ending in a consonant + <u>o</u>.	❏ Exercise 1: Spelling Pretest 1 ❏ Memorize It	❏ Exercise 2: Sort It: Syllable Types ❏ Word Fluency 1 ❏ Memorize It ❏ Handwriting Practice
STEP 3	**Vocabulary and Morphology** • Identify present participles acting as adjectives. • Identify antonyms, synonyms, and attributes. • Use the meaning of prefixes to define words.	❏ Unit Vocabulary ❏ Explore It (T) ❏ Expression of the Day	❏ Exercise 3: Sort It: Tense Timeline ❏ Exercise 4: Find It: Present Participles ❏ Expression of the Day
STEP 4	**Grammar and Usage** • Identify nouns and adjectives. • Identify prepositions and prepositional phrases. • Identify **have** as a main or helping verb. • Write sentences with a compound direct object.	❏ Exercise 2: Identify It: Noun, Adjective, or Other	❏ Exercise 5: Identify It: Prepositional Phrases
STEP 5	**Listening and Reading Comprehension** • Use context-based strategies to define words. • Identify signal words for comprehension: **use, generalize, infer, show**. • Identify main idea and details. • Identify transition words in informational text organized by time sequence and classification. • Answer comprehension questions.	❏ Exercise 3: Phrase It ❏ Independent Text: "Mythical Heroes"	❏ Exercise 6: Find It: Open Syllables ❏ Passage Fluency 1 ❏ Exercise 7: Use the Clues
STEP 6	**Speaking and Writing** • Organize main ideas and details for writing. • Apply outline to writing a summary paragraph. • Use transition words for time sequence and classification paragraphs.	❏ Masterpiece Sentences: Stages 1–3 ❏ Sentence Types: Fact or Opinion?	❏ Exercise 8: Rewrite It: Pronouns
	Self-Evaluation (5 is the highest) **Effort** = I produced my best work. **Participation** = I was actively involved in tasks. **Independence** = I worked on my own.	**Effort:** 1 2 3 4 5 **Participation:** 1 2 3 4 5 **Independence:** 1 2 3 4 5	**Effort:** 1 2 3 4 5 **Participation:** 1 2 3 4 5 **Independence:** 1 2 3 4 5
	Teacher Evaluation	**Effort:** 1 2 3 4 5 **Participation:** 1 2 3 4 5 **Independence:** 1 2 3 4 5	**Effort:** 1 2 3 4 5 **Participation:** 1 2 3 4 5 **Independence:** 1 2 3 4 5

Lesson 3 (Date:_____)	Lesson 4 (Date:_____)	Lesson 5 (Date:_____)
❑ Syllable Awareness: Deletion	❑ Exercise 1: Syllable Awareness: Segmentation	❑ Content Mastery: Syllable Awareness
❑ Exercise 1: Sort It: Syllable Types ❑ Exercise 2: Find It: Essential Words ❑ Word Fluency 1	❑ Exercise 2: Divide It ❑ Two-Syllable Words ❑ Word Fluency 2 ❑ Type It: Essential Words	❑ Content Mastery: Spelling Posttest 1
❑ Exercise 3: Define It ❑ Draw It: Idioms ❑ Expression of the Day	❑ Exercise 3: Identify It: Function of -ing ❑ Expression of the Day	❑ Exercise 1: Word Networks: Antonyms, Synonyms, and Attributes ❑ Draw It: Idioms ❑ Expression of the Day
❑ Introduction: The Verb *Have* ❑ Exercise 4: Identify It: *Have*—Main Verb or Helping Verb ❑ Exercise 5: Identify It: *Have*—Verb Tense	❑ Exercise 4: Find It: Forms of *Have* ❑ Exercise 5: Identify It: Irregular Verb Forms ❑ Exercise 6: Find It: Irregular Verbs	❑ Masterpiece Sentences: All Stages ❑ Identify It: Complete Subject and Complete Predicate
❑ Instructional Text: "Legendary Superheroes" ❑ Exercise 6: Use the Clues	❑ Instructional Text: "Legendary Superheroes" ❑ Exercise 7: Blueprint for Reading: Main Ideas, Details, Transition Words (T)	❑ Explore It (T)
❑ Exercise 7: Answer It	❑ Write It: Topic Sentence ❑ Exercise 8: Blueprint for Writing: Outline (T) ❑ Challenge Text: "Navajo Code Talkers"	❑ Write It: Summary (T) ❑ Challenge Text: "Navajo Code Talkers"
Effort: 1 2 3 4 5 **Participation:** 1 2 3 4 5 **Independence:** 1 2 3 4 5	**Effort:** 1 2 3 4 5 **Participation:** 1 2 3 4 5 **Independence:** 1 2 3 4 5	**Effort:** 1 2 3 4 5 **Participation:** 1 2 3 4 5 **Independence:** 1 2 3 4 5
Effort: 1 2 3 4 5 **Participation:** 1 2 3 4 5 **Independence:** 1 2 3 4 5	**Effort:** 1 2 3 4 5 **Participation:** 1 2 3 4 5 **Independence:** 1 2 3 4 5	**Effort:** 1 2 3 4 5 **Participation:** 1 2 3 4 5 **Independence:** 1 2 3 4 5

Check off the activities you complete with each lesson. Evaluate your accomplishments at the end of each lesson. Pay attention to teacher evaluations and comments.

Unit Objectives	Lesson 6 (Date:_____)	Lesson 7 (Date:_____)
STEP 1 **Phonemic Awareness and Phonics** • Segment and delete syllables from multisyllable words. • Say long vowel sounds for: <u>a</u>, <u>e</u>, <u>i</u>, <u>o</u>, <u>u</u>. • Identify **open** syllables. • Identify stressed syllables.	❑ Exercise 1: Listening for Stressed Syllables	❑ Exercise 1: Listening for Stressed Syllables
STEP 2 **Word Recognition and Spelling** • Read and spell words with **open** syllables. • Read and spell the **Essential Words**: *good, great, right, though, through, year.* • Spell words with prefixes: **pre-, re-, super-**. • Read and spell contractions with **have**. • Add **-es** to words ending in a consonant + <u>o</u>.	❑ Exercise 2: Spelling Pretest 2 ❑ Word Fluency 3	❑ Exercise 2: Divide It ❑ Exercise 3: Find It: Contractions ❑ Exercise 4: Build It: Prefixed Words
STEP 3 **Vocabulary and Morphology** • Identify present participles acting as adjectives. • Identify antonyms, synonyms, and attributes. • Use the meaning of prefixes to define words.	❑ Unit Vocabulary ❑ Exercise 3: Word Networks: Antonyms, Synonyms, and Attributes ❑ Expression of the Day	❑ Introduction: Prefixes **pre-, re-, super-** ❑ Exercise 5: Define It: Prefixes ❑ Expression of the Day
STEP 4 **Grammar and Usage** • Identify nouns and adjectives. • Identify prepositions and prepositional phrases. • Identify **have** as a main or helping verb. • Write sentences with a compound direct object.	❑ Exercise 4: Combine It: Compound Direct Objects	❑ Exercise 6: Diagram It: Compound Direct Objects (T)
STEP 5 **Listening and Reading Comprehension** • Use context-based strategies to define words. • Identify signal words for comprehension: **use, generalize, infer, show**. • Identify main idea and details. • Identify transition words in informational text organized by time sequence and classification. • Answer comprehension questions.	❑ Exercise 5: Phrase It ❑ Independent Text: "Unsung Heroes" ❑ Exercise 6: Use the Clues	❑ Passage Fluency 2 ❑ Exercise 7: Use the Clues
STEP 6 **Speaking and Writing** • Organize main ideas and details for writing. • Apply outline to writing a summary paragraph. • Use transition words for time sequence and classification paragraphs.	❑ Exercise 7: Rewrite It: Pronouns	❑ Exercise 8: Rewrite It: Pronouns
Self-Evaluation (5 is the highest) **Effort** = I produced my best work. **Participation** = I was actively involved in tasks. **Independence** = I worked on my own.	**Effort:** 1 2 3 4 5 **Participation:** 1 2 3 4 5 **Independence:** 1 2 3 4 5	**Effort:** 1 2 3 4 5 **Participation:** 1 2 3 4 5 **Independence:** 1 2 3 4 5
Teacher Evaluation	**Effort:** 1 2 3 4 5 **Participation:** 1 2 3 4 5 **Independence:** 1 2 3 4 5	**Effort:** 1 2 3 4 5 **Participation:** 1 2 3 4 5 **Independence:** 1 2 3 4 5

Lesson 8 (Date:_____)	**Lesson 9** (Date:_____)	**Lesson 10** (Date:_____)
❑ Exercise 1: Listening for Word Parts	❑ Exercise 1: Listening for Stressed Syllables	❑ Exercise 1: Listening for Stressed Syllables
❑ Exercise 2: Sort It: Words Ending in **o** ❑ Word Fluency 4	❑ Exercise 2: Find It: Words Ending in **o** ❑ Exercise 3: Build It	❑ Content Mastery: Spelling Posttest 2
❑ Content Mastery: Word Relationships ❑ Content Mastery: Morphology	❑ Prefixes: **pre-, re-, super-** ❑ Exercise 4: Define It: Prefixes ❑ Expression of the Day	❑ Exercise 2: Find It: Prefixed Words ❑ Exercise 3: Sort It: Prefixed Words ❑ Draw It: Idioms ❑ Expression of the Day
❑ Exercise 3: Sentence Dictation ❑ Masterpiece Sentences: Stage 2 (T)	❑ Exercise 5: Revise It: Compound Direct Objects	❑ Content Mastery: *Have*—Main Verb or Helping Verb ❑ Content Mastery: Prepositions ❑ Content Mastery: Compound Direct Objects
❑ Instructional Text: "These Shoes of Mine"	❑ Instructional Text: "These Shoes of Mine" ❑ Spotlight on Characters: Act It	❑ Content Mastery: Answering Questions ❑ Spotlight on Characters: Character Interview
❑ Exercise 4: Answer It	❑ Exercise 6: Answer It ❑ Challenge Text: "The Ride of Her Life"	❑ Exercise 4: Reflect and Respond ❑ Challenge Text: "The Ride of Her Life"
Effort: 1 2 3 4 5 **Participation:** 1 2 3 4 5 **Independence:** 1 2 3 4 5	**Effort:** 1 2 3 4 5 **Participation:** 1 2 3 4 5 **Independence:** 1 2 3 4 5	**Effort:** 1 2 3 4 5 **Participation:** 1 2 3 4 5 **Independence:** 1 2 3 4 5
Effort: 1 2 3 4 5 **Participation:** 1 2 3 4 5 **Independence:** 1 2 3 4 5	**Effort:** 1 2 3 4 5 **Participation:** 1 2 3 4 5 **Independence:** 1 2 3 4 5	**Effort:** 1 2 3 4 5 **Participation:** 1 2 3 4 5 **Independence:** 1 2 3 4 5

Exercise 1 · Spelling Pretest 1

▸ Write the words your teacher repeats.

1. _____

2. _____

3. _____

4. _____

5. _____

6. _____

7. _____

8. _____

9. _____

10. _____

11. _____

12. _____

13. _____

14. _____

15. _____

Exercise 2 · Identify It: Noun, Adjective, or Other

▸ Read the examples with your teacher.

▸ Use the context to decide if the underlined word is a noun, adjective, or other.

▸ Finish the rest of the sentences independently.

▸ Discuss the answers.

Examples:	Noun	Adjective	Other
<u>Superheroes</u> fill comic strips.	X		
Heroes have <u>superhuman</u> skills.		X	
Heroes can <u>inspire</u> us.			X

	Noun	Adjective	Other
1. Myths are made up of <u>tales</u>.			
2. <u>Early</u> people believed in myths.			
3. <u>Humans</u> wanted to understand their world.			
4. In myths, different gods <u>ruled</u> the world.			
5. <u>Romans</u> had many gods.			
6. Saturn was a <u>Roman</u> god.			
7. Juno <u>was</u> the goddess of husbands and wives.			
8. The <u>strongest</u> god was Jupiter.			
9. Neptune decided the <u>fate</u> of ships.			
10. Pluto ruled a dark and <u>grim</u> world.			

Unit 15 · Lesson 1

Exercise 3 · Phrase It

▸ Using the penciling strategy to "scoop" the phrases in each sentence.

▸ Read the sentences as you would speak them.

▸ The first two are done for you.

1. Superheroes fill comic strips.

2. They have superhuman skills.

3. They ensure that good wins over evil.

4. Heroes can give us hope.

5. Humans wanted to make sense of their world.

6. They made up tales to explain their world.

7. These tales are called myths.

8. People lived as if myths were based in fact.

9. These myths are still told.

10. Nobody believes them anymore.

Exercise 1 · Listening for Sounds in Words

▶ Listen to each word your teacher says.

▶ Identify the vowel sound in the first syllable of each word.

▶ Write the letter for the vowel sound and its diacritical mark on the line.

1. _____   2. _____   3. _____   4. _____   5. _____

6. _____   7. _____   8. _____   9. _____   10. _____

Exercise 2 · Sort It: Syllable Types

▶ Read the words in the **Word Bank**.

▶ Sort the words according to their syllable type.

▶ Write each word under the correct heading.

Word Bank

corn	long	star	pen
we	press	be	or
her	me	gal	men

closed	r-controlled	open

Unit 15 · Lesson 2

Exercise 3 · Sort It: Tense Timeline

▸ Read each sentence.

▸ Decide if **-ing** in the underlined verb phrase is signaling ongoing action in the past, present, or future.

▸ Record the verb phrase on the timeline in the correct column.

1. Heroes <u>were inspiring</u> us.

2. They <u>are giving</u> us hope.

3. Humans <u>are striving</u> to understand conflict.

4. They <u>will be giving</u> us hope.

5. Humans <u>were making</u> up tales.

Yesterday	Today	Tomorrow
Past	Present	Future

Exercise 4 · Find It: Present Participles

▸ Read each sentence.

▸ Circle the present participle that acts as an adjective.

▸ Underline the noun that the present participle describes.

1. We saw the erupting volcano.

2. The ringing bell signaled a tornado.

3. Their defending champ is the hero.

4. The overlapping files were deleted.

5. Caring heroes are popular human beings.

Exercise 5 · Identify It: Prepositional Phrases

▸ Read each sentence and the underlined prepositional phrase.

▸ Circle the preposition.

▸ Decide if the preposition shows position in space or time.

▸ Record the preposition in the correct column.

1. In comic books, superheroes do amazing deeds.

2. Inside their dwellings, parents told children the myths.

3. Ships sailed across the sea on calm days.

4. Ships did not sail during storms.

5. Neptune was blamed when ships crashed against the rock.

6. After a storm, Neptune would calm the waves.

7. A trip into Pluto's kingdom was dark and scary.

8. Juno stood by Jupiter's side as his wife.

9. Mythical heroes ruled over the world.

10. Before scientific facts, humans believed myths to be true.

Positions in Space	Positions in Time

Exercise 6 · Find It: Open Syllables

▸ Read the text.

▸ Highlight words with **open syllables**.

▸ Sort and record the open-syllable words according to their long vowel sounds.

> **from "Mythical Heroes"**
>
> They fill comic strips. They have superhuman skills. They're strong,
> quick, talented, and wise. They ensure that good wins over evil. Who
> are these superhumans? Superheroes! We all love heroes. Heroes can
> inspire us. They can give us hope. Do you have a hero?

/ $\bar{a}$ /	/ $\bar{e}$ /	/ $\bar{o}$ /	/ $\overline{oo}$ /

Unit 15 · Lesson 2

Exercise 7 · Use the Clues

▸ Read the sentence pairs.

▸ Read the pronoun that is circled.

▸ Identify the noun that the pronoun replaces in each sentence.

▸ Draw an arrow to show the link between the pronoun and the noun it replaced.

▸ Underline the noun that was replaced by the pronoun.

1. Jupiter was the king of the gods. (He) was the strongest god.

2. Juno was his wife. (She) was the goddess of husbands and wives.

3. Neptune ruled the seas. (He) held the fate of ships in his hands.

4. It was Neptune's choice. (His) brother, Pluto, ruled over the dead.

5. Neptune's brother, Pluto, ruled the land. (His) kingdom was a dark and grim land.

Exercise 8 · Rewrite It: Pronouns

▸ Reread each pair of sentences in Exercise 7, **Use the Clues**.

▸ Replace the pronoun with the noun that it represents.

▸ Rewrite the sentence using the noun.

▸ Check for sentence signals—capital letters, commas, and end punctuation.

▸ Read the new sentence.

▸ Do the first one with your teacher.

1. _____

2. _____

3. _____

4. _____

5. _____

Exercise 1 · Sort It: Syllable Types

▸ Read the words in the **Word Bank**.

▸ Sort syllables in the V/CV words according to their syllable type.

▸ Write each syllable under the correct heading.

▸ Say the syllables with your teacher.

Word Bank

acorn	equal	legal	tiger	music
debug	fever	moment	secret	silent

closed	r-controlled	open

Exercise 2 · Find It: Essential Words

▸ Find the **Essential Words** for this unit in these sentences.

▸ Underline them. There may be more than one in a sentence.

1. I am good at fixing equipment.

2. That was great music in the park.

3. Turn right at the next block.

4. She's only one year old though.

5. We drove through a secret tunnel.

▸ Write the **Essential Words** in the spaces.

_____   _____   _____

_____   _____   _____

Unit 15 · Lesson 3

Exercise 3 · Define It

▶ Fill in the blanks with a category and an attribute to define the word.

▶ Compare definitions that you're unsure of with a dictionary definition.

▶ Do the first word with your teacher.

1. A **hero** is _____ who is _____
                                 category   **attribute(s)**

   _____

   _____ .

2. A **human** is _____ who _____
                                    category   **attribute(s)**

   _____

   _____ .

3. A **lion** is _____ that is _____

   _____

   _____ .

4. A **pilot** is _____ who _____

   _____

   _____ .

5. A **spider** is _____ that _____

   _____

   _____ .

6. A **tiger** is _____ that _____

   _____

   _____ .

(continued)

Exercise 3 (continued) · Define It

7. **Zero** is _____ that _____

_____

_____ .

8. **Total** is _____ that _____

_____

_____ .

9. **Equal** is _____ that _____

_____

_____ .

10. A **poem** is _____ that _____

_____

_____ .

Which vocabulary words are related to mammals?

▸ Write the words in the blanks.

_____   _____   _____

_____   _____

Unit 15 · Lesson 3

Exercise 4 · Identify It: *Have*—Main Verb or Helping Verb

▸ Use the **Forms of Be, Have, and Do** chart in the back of the *Student Text* to identify the form of the verb **have** in the following sentences.

▸ Underline the form of the verb **have** that you find in each sentence.

▸ Fill in the bubble to show if the form of **have** is used as a main verb or helping verb.

	Main Verb	Helping Verb
1. We have hope.	◯	◯
2. She has learned about myths.	◯	◯
3. He will have a vacation later.	◯	◯
4. You have passed the test.	◯	◯
5. I have been ill.	◯	◯

Exercise 5 · Identify It: *Have*—Verb Tense

▸ Use the **Forms of Be, Have, and Do** chart in the back of the *Student Text* to identify the form of **have** in these sentences.

▸ Circle the verb **have**.

▸ Fill in the bubble to show if the verb **have** is in the past, present, or future tense.

	Past	Present	Future
1. We will have lunch later.	◯	◯	◯
2. The superhero had saved the day.	◯	◯	◯
3. He has a great bike.	◯	◯	◯
4. They had chosen great music.	◯	◯	◯
5. I will have finished the project tomorrow.	◯	◯	◯

Exercise 6 · Use the Clues

▸ Circle the vocabulary word **exaggerated**.

▸ Discuss the definition of **exaggerated** with your teacher. **Exaggerated** means *to overstate something* or *to say something is better, worse, more important, etc., than it really is.*

▸ **Example:** His three-pound fish became a twenty-pound fish when he retold the story later around the campfire.

Underline two examples in the excerpt below that illustrate the word **exaggerated**.

> ### from "Legendary Superheroes"
>
> This isn't just the plot of an action-packed film. It's a story that's been told again and again. It's been told since people first began to entertain each other by making up stories. The stories became legends. They started as tales about real people. But as the stories were passed on for many years, they became more and more exaggerated. A fight against three people turned into a battle against ten. Eventually, there were 100 fearsome enemies! A favorite weapon became an invincible magic tool. The superheroes described in these stories can be identified by a variety of traits.

Exercise 7 · Answer It

▸ Underline the signal word in each question.

▸ Write the answer in complete sentences.

▸ Check for sentence signals—capital letters, commas, and end punctuation.

1. Infer what happened when Odysseus' men jumped out from hiding in the wooden horse.

   _____

   _____

   _____

   _____

2. Explain what the author meant about *quests* in the statement, "But for a hero, that's all in a day's work!" (lines 76–77)

   _____

   _____

   _____

   _____

3. List the characteristics of superheroes.

   _____

   _____

   _____

   _____

(continued)

4. Use ideas from this text selection to create your own superhero. Be sure to include: a name, superpowers, examples of heroic deeds, and one weakness.

_____

_____

_____

_____

5. The stories of some of these legendary superheroes come from myths. Name the mythical Greek heroes mentioned in this article. Do you think any of them were real people? Why or why not?

_____

_____

_____

_____

Exercise 1 · Syllable Awareness: Segmentation

▸ Listen to the word your teacher says.

▸ Count the syllables. Write the number in the first column.

▸ Write the letter for each vowel sound you hear.

▸ Mark each short vowel with a breve (˘).

▸ Mark each long vowel with a macron (‾).

	How many syllables do you hear?	First vowel sound	Second vowel sound	Third vowel sound
1.				
2.				
3.				
4.				
5.				

Exercise 2 · Divide It

▸ Follow along with your teacher's example.

▸ Use the steps of **Divide It Checklist** to break the words into syllables.

▸ Rewrite each word.

▸ Mark each short vowel with a breve (˘).

▸ Mark each long vowel with a macron (¯).

▸ Blend the syllables together to read the entire word.

1. music

2. donut

3. basin

4. hotel

5. unit

Unit 15 · Lesson 4

Exercise 3 · Identify It: Function of -ing

▸ Read the examples with your teacher.

▸ Use context to decide if each underlined word is a present participle acting as an adjective or as an ongoing action (verb).

▸ Discuss the answers.

Example:	Adjective	Ongoing Action Verb
<u>Opening</u> night was a huge success.		
He <u>is opening</u> his gifts with care.		

▸ Read the rest of the sentences independently.

▸ Decide the function of the underlined present participle.

▸ Mark the correct answer.

	Adjective	Ongoing Action Verb
1. The <u>returning</u> hero was welcomed.		
2. The hero <u>was returning</u> to his family.		
3. He is a <u>beginning</u> judo student.		
4. I <u>am beginning</u> to understand.		
5. The <u>defending</u> champ will get even.		

Exercise 4 · Find It: Forms of *Have*

▸ Read each sentence.

▸ Underline the entire verb phrase and circle the form of **have**.

1. Early humans (had) created myths to explain their world.

2. Through the years, myths have been replaced by facts.

3. Researchers have proved many myths to be untrue.

4. In the future, people will have different heroes to inspire them.

5. Many plays have been written based on the tales in the myths.

6. The class had written their own myths about high school.

7. Throughout time myths have served a useful purpose.

8. Most people have seen superheroes in comic strips.

9. The toy industry has made superhero action figures.

10. Many children have collected different superheroes.

Unit 15 · Lesson 4

Exercise 5 · Identify It: Irregular Verb Forms

▸ Read the present tense verbs in the **Present** column in the chart below.

▸ Write the irregular past tense forms of the verbs in the **Past** column.

▸ The first one is done as an example.

	Present	Past
1.	have	had
2.	become	
3.	ride	
4.	begin	
5.	go	
6.	shine	
7.	forget	
8.	lend	
9.	write	
10.	bring	

Exercise 6 · Find It: Irregular Verbs

▸ Read the following passage adapted from **"Mythical Heroes."**

▸ Underline the irregular past tense verbs.

Hint: There are ten.

---

based on "Mythical Heroes"

Early humans told myths to explain their world. The gods were the superheroes of the myths. They had great power.

Neptune made the seas still. He held the fate of ships in his hands.

Pluto was the ruler of the dark kingdom. He led the dead into the afterlife. He went into the underworld. Jupiter became the ruler of the gods. He gave orders to the other gods.

Exercise 7 · Blueprint for Reading: Main Ideas, Details, Transition Words

▸ Read the excerpt from **"Legendary Superheroes."**

▸ Circle the transition words.

▸ Highlight in blue the main ideas.

▸ Highlight in pink details about each main idea.

---

from "Legendary Superheroes"

Superstrength

First of all, most legendary heroes have some kind of superhuman power. The heroes of ancient Greek legends were usually related to the gods. This meant that they would be extra strong, extra clever, and always have luck on their side. The best known of the Greek superheroes, Hercules, was only a baby when he strangled two snakes that had been sent to kill him!

(continued)

Magic Powers

Also, some superheroes use magic. One example is Odin. He was the Vikings' most important god. He had an invincible spear called *Gungnir.* He also had two ravens. They would perch on his shoulders and fly off to spy on his enemies. His son, Thor, had a hammer called *Mjolnir* ("the destroyer"). The hammer returned like a boomerang whenever he threw it. Thor also had a magic belt. This belt doubled his strength.

Fatal Flaw

In addition, some superheroes have a fatal flaw. Few heroes are totally invincible. Most have one weakness that can destroy them. With Superman, it was a mineral, kryptonite. In the case of Achilles, the great Greek warrior of the Trojan War, it was his heel. When Achilles was a baby, his mother dipped him in the magic river Styx. This made his whole body invulnerable—except the heel by which he was held. He finally died when a poisoned arrow struck him on the heel. (Today, we still say a person's weak point is an Achilles' heel.)

(continued)

Exercise 7 *(continued)* · Blueprint for Reading: Main Ideas, Details, Transition Words

Taste for Adventure

Finally, some superheroes participate in quests. When they're not saving the world, many superheroes go on quests. These are long, dangerous journeys. The objective of a quest is to search for a special place or object. King Arthur's knights, for example, went on a quest to find the Holy Grail, a sacred cup. In a quest, a hero faces many perils and challenges. These test strength, courage, and honor to the very limits. But for a hero, that's all in a day's work!

Exercise 8 · Blueprint for Writing: Outline

▸ Use the highlighted text for Exercise 7, **Blueprint for Reading**, to complete the outline.

▸ Write the topic sentence on the first line.

▸ Write the main ideas on the lines beginning with Roman numerals.

▸ Write the details about each main idea on the lines beginning with letters.

▸ Add the transition words to the outline by drawing circles in the margins next to the main ideas. Write the transition words inside the circles.

▸ Write a conclusion sentence.

_____

I. _____

    A. _____

    B. _____

    C. _____

    D. _____

II. _____

    A. _____

    B. _____

    C. _____

    D. _____

(continued)

Exercise 8 (continued) · Blueprint for Writing: Outline

III. _____

    A. _____

    B. _____

    C. _____

    D. _____

IV. _____

    A. _____

    B. _____

    C. _____

    D. _____

_____

Exercise 1 · Word Networks: Antonyms, Synonyms, and Attributes

Antonyms

▸ Read the words in the **Word Bank**.

▸ Choose and write the word from the **Word Bank** that is an antonym (opposite).

▸ Read the word pairs. Discuss your answers.

Word Bank

good	after	close
odd	remember	equal

1. before: _____

2. open: _____

3. forget: _____

4. even: _____

5. evil: _____

Synonyms

▸ Read the words in the **Word Bank**.

▸ Choose and write the word from the **Word Bank** that is a synonym (same or almost the same).

▸ Read the word pairs. Discuss your answers.

Word Bank

equal	prior	silent
odd	start	zero

(continued)

Exercise 1 (continued) · Word Networks: Antonyms, Synonyms, and Attributes

6. none: _____

7. quiet: _____

8. same: _____

9. begin: _____

10. before: _____

Attributes

▸ Read the words in the **Word Bank**.

▸ Choose and write the word from the **Word Bank** that is an attribute.

▸ Read the word pairs. Discuss your answers.

Word Bank

equal	zero	wind
bravery	cart	facts

11. tornado: _____

12. report: _____

13. supermarket: _____

14. hero: _____

15. hundred: _____

Exercise 1 · Listening for Stressed Syllables

▸ Listen to each word your teacher says. Repeat the word.

▸ Listen for the stressed syllable.

▸ Make an X in the box to mark the position of the stressed syllable.

	1st Syllable	2nd Syllable	3rd Syllable
1. omit			
2. minor			
3. represent			
4. elastic			
5. overly			
6. lumbago			
7. resulted			
8. unison			
9. indirect			
10. kimono			

Unit 15 · Lesson 6

Exercise 2 · Spelling Pretest 2

▸ Listen to the word your teacher repeats.

▸ Write the word.

1. _____

2. _____

3. _____

4. _____

5. _____

6. _____

7. _____

8. _____

9. _____

10. _____

11. _____

12. _____

13. _____

14. _____

15. _____

Exercise 3 · Word Networks: Antonyms, Synonyms, and Attributes

▸ Read each pair of words.

▸ Sort word pairs according to their relationship.

▸ Write the word pairs in the correct columns.

▸ Discuss answers with a partner.

even: odd	before: prior	quiet: silent	same: equal
supermarket: cart	evil: good	tornado: wind	forget: remember
open: close	begin: start	report: facts	hero: brave

Antonyms (opposite)	Synonyms (same)	Attributes

Exercise 4 · Combine It: Compound Direct Objects

▸ Read each pair of sentences with your teacher.

▸ Underline the direct object in each sentence.

▸ Use the conjunction given to combine the direct objects into a new sentence.

▸ Write the new sentence.

▸ Check for sentence signals—capital letters and end punctuation.

▸ Circle the compound direct objects.

1. Police find clues to solve a crime.
   Police find evidence to solve a crime.

or _____

2. The police arrested one suspect.
   The police did not arrest the other.

but _____

3. Some men and women join the army.
   Some join the air force.

or _____

4. Fires burn forests.
   Fires burn houses.

and _____

5. Soldiers fight the enemy.
   Soldiers do not fight friendly forces.

but _____

Exercise 5 · Phrase It

▸ Use the penciling strategy to "scoop" the phrases in each sentence.

▸ Read as you would speak them.

▸ The first two are done for you.

1. Unsung heroes risk their lives.

2. Firefighters are unsung heroes.

3. Men and women join the military.

4. Soldiers watch over the homelands.

5. Soldiers expect nothing in return.

6. The police are there to help.

7. Police work makes our lives safer.

8. Police help solve crimes.

9. Soldiers and firefighters are unsung heroes.

10. The police are unsung heroes.

Unit 15 · Lesson 6

Exercise 6 · Use the Clues

▸ Read each set of sentences.

▸ Find the pronoun that is circled.

▸ Underline the noun that the pronoun replaces.

▸ Draw an arrow to show the link between the pronoun and the noun it replaced.

1. Not all heroes are superheroes. (Some) spend their lives helping others.

2. Think of firefighters. Think of soldiers. Think of the police. (These) are the unsung heroes.

3. A call to 911 is a call to save lives. (It) is your direct line to the unsung heroes.

4. Men and women join the military. (They) watch over the homeland.

5. Our soldiers expect nothing in return. We should have pride in (them).

Exercise 7 · Rewrite It: Pronouns

▸ Read each sentence pair in Exercise 6: **Use the Clues**.

▸ Replace the circled pronoun with the noun that it represents.

▸ Rewrite the sentence using the noun.

▸ Check for sentence signals—capital letters, commas, and end punctuation.

▸ Read the new sentence.

1. _____

2. _____

3. _____

4. _____

5. _____

Exercise 1 · Listening for Stressed Syllables

▸ Listen to each word your teacher says. Repeat the word.

▸ Listen for the stressed, or accented, syllable.

▸ Make an X in the box to mark the position of the stressed syllable.

1. □□   6. □□

2. □□   7. □□

3. □□   8. □□

4. □□   9. □□

5. □□   10. □□

Exercise 2 · Divide It

▸ Follow along with your teacher's example.

▸ Use the steps of **Divide It** to break the words into syllables.

▸ Blend the syllables together to read the entire word.

lion	poem	fuel
liar	prior	riot

Exercise 3 · Find It: Contractions

▸ Read the sentences.

▸ Circle the contraction in each sentence.

▸ Expand each contraction into two words.

1. They've remembered the heroes with a poem.

2. We've fed the lion a good diet.

3. I've been out of fuel.

4. You've just missed the tornadoes!

5. They get zeroes if they're late.

1. _____

2. _____

3. _____

4. _____

5. _____

Exercise 4 · Build It: Prefixed Words

▸ Read the prefixes and word parts in the box.

▸ Combine the prefixes and word parts to make new words.

▸ Record the words under the correct headings.

▸ Check a dictionary to verify that words are real words.

re-	fix	order	hero
pre-	do	fab	fine
super-	shrunk	market	turn

re-	pre-	super-

Exercise 5 · Define It: Prefixes

▸ Complete each sentence by adding the meaning of the underlined word.

▸ Define the common prefix used in each set.

▸ Use a dictionary if you need help.

1. When you have to **<u>redo</u>** your homework, you have to _____.

2. When you have to **<u>reorder</u>** a stereo, you have to _____.

3. When you have to **<u>return</u>** home, you have to _____ home.

> **Re-** is a prefix that means _____.

4. A **<u>prefix</u>** is a word part that you fix or put _____.

5. A **<u>prefab</u>** house is built _____.

6. A **<u>preshrunk</u>** skirt is shrunk _____.

> **Pre-** is a prefix that means _____.

7. A **<u>superrich</u>** person is _____ rich.

8. A **<u>superhero</u>** is a hero who is _____ "ordinary" heroes.

9. A **<u>supermarket</u>** is a _____ where you buy food.

10. A **<u>superfine</u>** diamond is _____ ordinary diamonds.

> **Super-** is a prefix that means _____.

Unit 15 · Lesson 7

Exercise 6 · Diagram It: Compound Direct Objects

▸ Diagram the first sentence in the exercise with your teacher.

▸ Diagram the remaining compound direct object sentences independently.

▸ Write an X above the vertical line that separates the complete subject and the complete predicate.

    1. Police stop crime and misconduct.

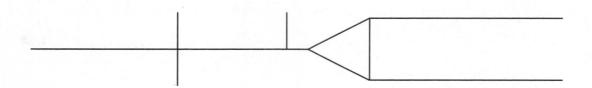

    2. The police enforce traffic rules and safety regulations.

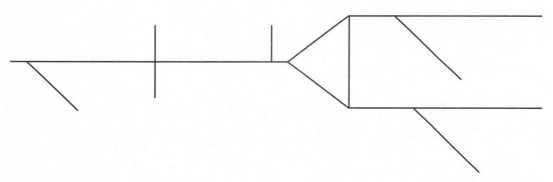

(*continued*)

Exercise 6 (continued) · Diagram It: Compound Direct Objects

3. Forest rangers monitor national parks and remote areas for fires.

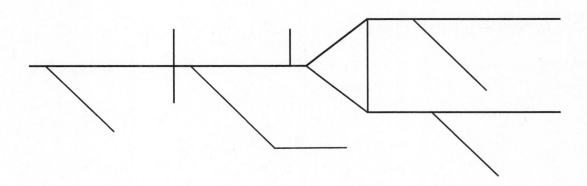

4. They relay messages or information to firefighters.

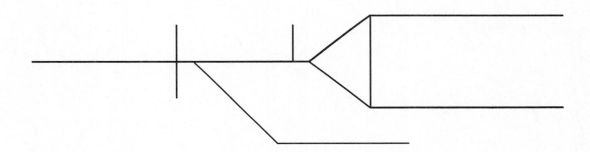

5. Soldiers also defend our country and its people.

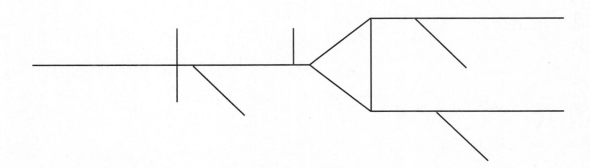

Exercise 7 · Use the Clues

▸ Read the passage.

▸ Read the circled pronouns.

▸ Underline the noun that the pronoun replaces.

▸ Draw an arrow to the word(s) it represents.

from "Unsung Heroes"

Crime is a big problem. (It) is everywhere. Some people shoplift. Some
use drugs. Some are reckless drivers. Some harm others. The police
are there to help. (They) bring back order. (They) help solve crimes.
(Their) work makes our lives safer. Like soldiers and fire fighters, (they)
are unsung heroes.

Exercise 8 · Rewrite It: Pronouns

▸ Reread the passage in Exercise 7, **Use the Clues**.

▸ Rewrite the underlined sentences, replacing the pronoun with a noun that it represents.

▸ Check for sentence signals—capital letters, commas, and end punctuation.

▸ Read your sentences to a partner.

1. _____

2. _____

3. _____

4. _____

5. _____

Exercise 1 · Listening for Word Parts

▶ Listen to each word your teacher says.

▶ Mark **Yes** or **No** to show whether or not the word has a suffix.

▶ If **Yes**, write the suffix.

	Do you hear a suffix on the word?		If **Yes**, what is the suffix?
	Yes	No	
1.			
2.			
3.			
4.			
5.			
6.			
7.			
8.			
9.			
10.			

Exercise 2 · Sort It: Words Ending in <u>o</u>

▸ Read the words in the **Word Bank**.

▸ Work in small groups or with a partner.

▸ Sort the words according to a spelling or syllable pattern.

  Hint: Notice what comes before the final <u>o</u> in each word.

▸ Label the headings.

Word Bank

heroes	tornadoes	videos	stereos
radios	zeroes	potatoes	goes

Unit 15 · Lesson 8

Exercise 3 · Sentence Dictation

▸ Write the sentences that your teacher dictates.

▸ Check that each sentence uses sentence signals—correct capitalization and end punctuation.

▸ Choose one sentence for use with the next activity, **Masterpiece Sentences**.

1. _____

2. _____

3. _____

4. _____

5. _____

Exercise 4 · Answer It

▸ Underline the signal word in the question.

▸ Write the answers in complete sentences.

▸ Check for sentence signals—capital letters, commas, and end punctuation.

(continued)

Exercise 4 (continued) · Answer It

1. Use drawings to show the expressions of Manuel's mood change from the beginning to the end of the story. Then explain the mood change in words.

At the beginning of the story,

Manuel felt _____

because _____

_____

_____

At the end of the story,

Manuel felt _____

because _____

_____

_____

2. Describe the condition of Manuel's shoes at the beginning of the story.

_____

_____

_____

_____

_____

_____

3. Explain why Manuel is considered a hero at the end of the story.

_____

_____

_____

_____

(continued)

Exercise 4 *(continued)* · **Answer It**

4. Use information in the preface and **Explore It** chart for "hero" to describe someone in your life who is an everyday hero.

_____

_____

_____

_____

_____

_____

5. **"These Shoes of Mine"** is a drama. Explain how this type of writing is different from a story such as **"Podway Bound"** in Unit 13. Do you think a play is easier or harder to read? Why?

_____

_____

_____

_____

_____

_____

Exercise 1 · Listening for Stressed Syllables

▸ Listen to each word your teacher says. Repeat the word.

▸ Listen for the stressed syllable.

▸ Place an X in the box to mark the position of the stressed syllable.

	1st Syllable	2nd Syllable	3rd Syllable	4th Syllable
1. condo				
2. super				
3. remember				
4. respect				
5. reordering				
6. driver				
7. reviving				
8. paper				
9. republic				
10. stucco				

Unit 15 · Lesson 9

Exercise 2 · Find It: Words Ending in <u>o</u>

▸ Use your Spelling Lists from Lessons 6–10 in the *Student Text* to find base words that end with <u>o</u>.

▸ Write the base words in the first column.

▸ Add -<u>s</u> or -<u>es</u> to each word. Write the new words in the second column.

Hint: One word doesn't follow the rule. Use a dictionary to discover which word is an exception to the spelling rule.

▸ Circle the exception to the spelling rule.

1. _____   _____

2. _____   _____

3. _____   _____

Exercise 3 · Build It

▸ Combine prefixes in the middle square with word parts to form new words.

▸ **Example: re + charge = recharge**.

▸ Record each new word in the chart that follows according to its prefix.

▸ Use a dictionary to verify that you are building real words.

vise	pay	state
charge	inter- in- re- dis- super- pre-	ject
fer	scribe	cline

inter-	in-	re-	dis-	super-	pre-

Unit 15 · Lesson 9

Exercise 4 · Define It: Prefixes

▶ Read each **prefix** in the first column of the chart.

▶ Choose a definition from the definition box to complete the second column. Definitions may be used more than once.

▶ Write two words that begin with each prefix.

Hint: Sometimes it's easier to think of words first, and then recall the **prefix's** meaning.

Definition Box:

before	above, beyond, bigger	into	below
back, again	away, apart	not	between

Prefix	Definition	Example Word	Example Word
un-			
re-			
pre-			
super-			
in-			
inter-			
under-			
non-			
dis-			

Exercise 5 · Revise It: Compound Direct Objects

▸ Read the text.

▸ Reread the underlined sentences.

▸ Use a conjunction (**and/or/but**) to combine the direct objects.

▸ Write the new sentence on the corresponding numbered line in the text below.

▸ Reread the new text together with your teacher.

---

based on "Unsung Heroes"

Fire is a big problem. <u>Fires burn homes. Fires burn huge plots of land.</u> <u>Firefighters save lives. Firefighters save property.</u> Firefighters are unsung heroes.

The military protects our homelands. <u>Men and women join the army. Men and women join the navy.</u>

<u>Our soldiers and sailors deserve our thanks. Our soldiers and sailors deserve our gratitude.</u>

<u>We should have pride in them. We should have confidence in them.</u> People in the military are also unsung heroes.

Fire is a big problem. _____ .
                                        1

_____ . Firefighters are unsung heroes.
             2

The military protects our homelands. _____
                                                    3

_____
                             4

_____
                             5

People in the military are also unsung heroes.

Exercise 6 · Answer It

▸ Complete the Venn diagram with your teacher.

▸ List similarities and differences between the Spanish and English text.

THESE SHOES OF MINE	**Estos Zapatos Míos**
(Manuel paces back and forth in big clunky shoes while his mother sits at a table sewing patches onto a pair of pants.)	*(Manuel camina de un lado a otro dando golpetazos con unos zapatos demasiado grandes mientras su madre, sentada a la mesa, pone remiendos a un par de pantalones.)*
MANUEL (*indicating his shoes*): Look at them!	**MANUEL** (*señalando sus zapatos*): ¡Mira estos zapatos!
MOTHER: They're nice, *mi'jo.*	**MADRE:** Son bonitos, mi'jo.
MANUEL: Nice! They're too big! They're old! They're ugly. (*Stomps his feet.*) And can you hear them?	**MANUEL:** ¡Bonitos! ¡Son demasiado grandes! ¡Son viejos! ¡Son feos! (*pisa con fuerza*) ¿Y oyes como suenan?
MOTHER: They're like drums.	**MADRE:** Suenan como tambores.
(Manuel stomps louder.)	*(Manuel pisa aún más fuerte.)*
MOTHER: No, like congas.	**MADRE:** No, como congas.
MANUEL: Everyone will hear me. They'll laugh and say, "Here comes Manuel in his big ugly shoes."	**MANUEL:** Todo el mundo me oirá. Se van a reír. "Ahí viene Manuel con esos horribles zapatones".

(continued)

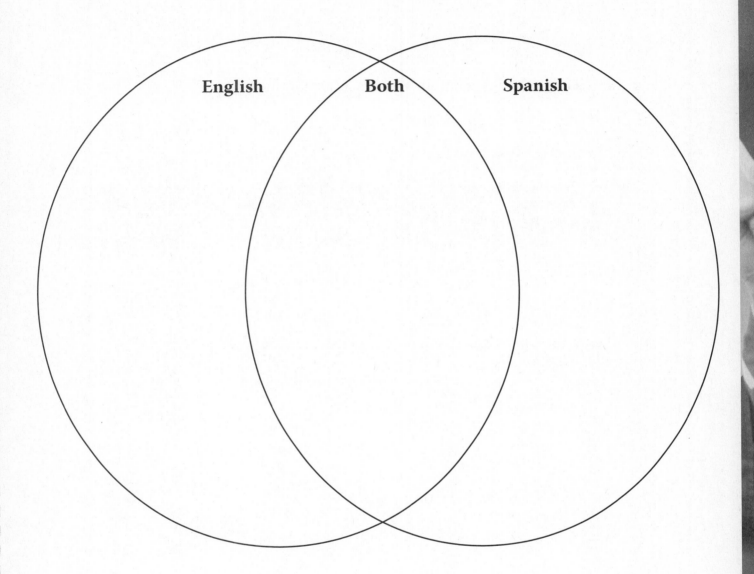

English   Both   Spanish

Exercise 1 · Listening for Stressed Syllables

▶ Listen to each word your teacher says.

▶ Count the syllables. Write the number in the first column.

▶ Say the word again. Listen for the stressed syllable.

▶ Write the letters for the stressed syllable in the correct column.

	How many syllables do you hear?	First Syllable	Second Syllable	Third Syllable
1.				
2.				
3.				
4.				
5.				
6.				
7.				
8.				
9				
10.				

Exercise 2 · Find It: Prefixed Words

▶ Read the following story with your teacher.

▶ Find and underline (or highlight) words with these prefixes: **pre-**, **super-**, **re-**, **dis-**, and **in-**.

The Repugnant Robots

Suddenly, a repugnant force of reviled alien robots invaded our unprepared world. They were sent by the inhabitants of a remote planet that had become superheated and was ready to disintegrate. The planet's inhabitants invented these superhuman robotic forms to invade our planet so they could remove us and take over. This distant superpower wanted to superimpose its will, reducing us humans to resemble worker ants forever under the robots' supervision. In short, we were in terrible danger. Little time remained! Was there anyone who could save the day? Someone strong, someone fearless—a hero! That could be you!

Unit 15 · Lesson 10

Exercise 3 · Sort It: Prefixed Words

▸ Sort the words from Exercise 2, **Find It: Prefixed Words,** by their prefixes.

▸ Write the words in the chart.

▸ Then answer the questions below.

pre-	super-	re-

in-	dis-	un-

▸ How many prefixes did you find? _____

▸ Look up **super-** words in the dictionary and collect some **super-** words that could describe your hero.

▸ Write a sentence using several of these **super-** words to describe the hero who came in at the last minute to save the world, as heroes often do.

_____

_____

Exercise 4 · Reflect and Respond

▸ Using the key points from the class discussion, write your response to the question below.

It was very important for Manuel to look good in front of his peers. Why do you think looking good seems to be more important to some people than telling the truth?

_____

_____

_____

_____

_____

_____

_____

_____

_____

_____

_____

_____

_____

_____

_____

_____

Check off the activities you complete with each lesson. Evaluate your accomplishments at the end of each lesson. Pay attention to teacher evaluations and comments.

Unit Objectives	Lesson 1 (Date:_____)	Lesson 2 (Date:_____)
STEP 1 — Phonemic Awareness and Phonics • Segment and delete syllables from multisyllable words. • Say long vowel sounds: <u>a</u>, <u>e</u>, <u>i</u>, <u>o</u>, <u>u</u>. • Identify final silent <u>e</u> syllables. • Identify stressed syllables.	❑ Phoneme Production/Replication ❑ Listening for Sounds in Words	❑ Introduction: Conditions for **Final Silent <u>e</u>** in Two-Syllable Words ❑ Exercise 1: Listening for Sounds in Words ❑ Listening for Sounds in Words
STEP 2 — Word Recognition and Spelling • Spell two-syllable words with **final silent <u>e</u>**. • Read and spell the **Essential Words**: *again, sound, today, tomorrow, want, work*. • Spell words with prefixes: **anti-, sub-**. • Read and spell contractions with **had** or **has**. • Use the **Drop <u>e</u> Rule**.	❑ Exercise 1: Spelling Pretest 1 ❑ Memorize It	❑ Exercise 2: Sort It: Syllable Types ❑ Word Fluency 1 ❑ Memorize It ❑ Handwriting Practice
STEP 3 — Vocabulary and Morphology • Identify past participles that act as adjectives. • Identify antonyms, synonyms, word attributes, and analogies. • Use the meaning of prefixes to define words.	❑ Unit Vocabulary ❑ Explore It (T) ❑ Expression of the Day	❑ Introduction: Past Participles ❑ Exercise 3: Find It: Past Participles ❑ Expression of the Day
STEP 4 — Grammar and Usage • Identify plural and possessive nouns and pronouns. • Identify prepositional phrases and object of the preposition. • Identify main verbs or helping verbs. • Write sentences with a compound adjective.	❑ Exercise 2: Identify It: Plural or Possessive ❑ Exercise 3: Find It: Possessives—Pronouns and Adjectives	❑ Exercise 4: Find It: Prepositional Phrases ❑ Exercise 5: Identify It: Object of the Preposition
STEP 5 — Listening and Reading Comprehension • Use context-based strategies to define words. • Identify signal words for comprehension: **distinguish, select**. • Identify main ideas.	❑ Exercise 4: Phrase It ❑ Independent Text: "The Complete Athlete"	❑ Exercise 6: Find It: Words With **Final Silent <u>e</u>** ❑ Passage Fluency 1 ❑ Exercise 7: Use the Clues
STEP 6 — Speaking and Writing • Organize main ideas for writing. • Apply outline to writing an introductory paragraph.	❑ Masterpiece Sentences: Stages 1–3 ❑ Sentence Types: Fact or Opinion?	❑ Exercise 8: Rewrite It: Pronouns
Self-Evaluation (5 is the highest) **Effort** = I produced my best work. **Participation** = I was actively involved in tasks. **Independence** = I worked on my own.	**Effort:** 1 2 3 4 5 **Participation:** 1 2 3 4 5 **Independence:** 1 2 3 4 5	**Effort:** 1 2 3 4 5 **Participation:** 1 2 3 4 5 **Independence:** 1 2 3 4 5
Teacher Evaluation	**Effort:** 1 2 3 4 5 **Participation:** 1 2 3 4 5 **Independence:** 1 2 3 4 5	**Effort:** 1 2 3 4 5 **Participation:** 1 2 3 4 5 **Independence:** 1 2 3 4 5

Lesson 3 (Date:_____)	Lesson 4 (Date:_____)	Lesson 5 (Date:_____)
❑ Phoneme Segmentation ❑ Phoneme Substitution ❑ Syllable Awareness: Segmentation ❑ Exercise 1: Listening for Sounds in Words	❑ Exercise 1: Syllable Awareness: Segmentation	❑ Content Mastery: Syllable Awareness
❑ Exercise 2: Divide It ❑ Exercise 3: Find It: Essential Words ❑ Word Fluency 1	❑ Drop It: **Drop e Rule** (T) ❑ Word Fluency 2 ❑ Type It: Essential Words ❑ Exercise 2: Build It: Prefixed Words	❑ Content Mastery: Spelling Posttest 1
❑ Exercise 4: Define It ❑ Draw It: Idioms ❑ Expression of the Day	❑ Introduction: Prefixes: **sub-** ❑ Exercise 3: Define It: Prefixed Words ❑ Exercise 4: Identify It: Suffixes **-ed** and **-en** ❑ Expression of the Day	❑ Unit Vocabulary ❑ Exercise 1: Word Networks: Antonyms, Synonyms, and Attributes ❑ Draw It: Idioms ❑ Expression of the Day
❑ Exercise 5: Identify It: Main Verb or Helping Verb	❑ Exercise 5: Rewrite It: Irregular Verb Forms ❑ Exercise 6: Find It: Irregular Past Tense	❑ Masterpiece Sentences: Stage 4: Paint Your Subject
❑ Instructional Text: "A Special Kind of Athlete" ❑ Exercise 6: Use the Clues	❑ Exercise 7: Blueprint for Reading: Identifying Main Ideas (T)	❑ Exercise 7: Blueprint for Reading: Identifying Main Ideas (T) (Lesson 4)
❑ Exercise 7: Answer It	❑ Exercise 8: Blueprint for Writing: Outline (T) ❑ Exercise 9: Paraphrase It ❑ Challenge Text: "Swifter, Higher, Stronger"	❑ Exercise 8: Blueprint for Writing: Outline (T) (Lesson 4) ❑ Exercise 2: Paraphrase It ❑ Exercise 3: Write It ❑ Challenge Text: "Swifter, Higher, Stronger"
Effort: 1 2 3 4 5 **Participation:** 1 2 3 4 5 **Independence:** 1 2 3 4 5	**Effort:** 1 2 3 4 5 **Participation:** 1 2 3 4 5 **Independence:** 1 2 3 4 5	**Effort:** 1 2 3 4 5 **Participation:** 1 2 3 4 5 **Independence:** 1 2 3 4 5
Effort: 1 2 3 4 5 **Participation:** 1 2 3 4 5 **Independence:** 1 2 3 4 5	**Effort:** 1 2 3 4 5 **Participation:** 1 2 3 4 5 **Independence:** 1 2 3 4 5	**Effort:** 1 2 3 4 5 **Participation:** 1 2 3 4 5 **Independence:** 1 2 3 4 5

Check off the activities you complete with each lesson. Evaluate your accomplishments at the end of each lesson. Pay attention to teacher evaluations and comments.

Unit Objectives	Lesson 6 (Date:_____)	Lesson 7 (Date:_____)
STEP 1 **Phonemic Awareness and Phonics** • Segment and delete syllables from multisyllable words. • Say long vowel sounds: a, e, i, o, u. • Identify **final silent e** syllables. • Identify stressed syllables.	❑ Exercise 1: Listening for Stressed Syllables	❑ Exercise 1: Listening for Word Parts ❑ Exercise 2: Listening for Stressed Syllables
STEP 2 **Word Recognition and Spelling** • Spell two-syllable words with **final silent e**. • Read and spell the **Essential Words**. • Spell words with prefixes: **anti-, sub-**. • Read and spell contractions with **have** or **has**. • Follow the **Drop e Rule**.	❑ Exercise 2: Spelling Pretest 2 ❑ Word Fluency 3	❑ Exercise 3: Divide It ❑ Exercise 4: Find It: Contractions ❑ Word Fluency 4
STEP 3 **Vocabulary and Morphology** • Identify past participles that act as adjectives. • Identify antonyms, synonyms, word attributes, and analogies. • Use the meaning of prefixes to define words.	❑ Introduction: Analogies ❑ Exercise 3: Word Networks: Analogies ❑ Expression of the Day	❑ Introduction: Prefix **anti-** ❑ Exercise 5: Define It ❑ Exercise 6: Find It: Past Participle Phrases ❑ Expression of the Day
STEP 4 **Grammar and Usage** • Identify plural and possessive nouns and pronouns. • Identify prepositional phrases and object of the preposition. • Identify main verbs or helping verbs. • Write sentences with a compound adjective.	❑ Introduction: Compound Adjectives ❑ Exercise 4: Find It: Compound Adjectives	❑ Exercise 7: Diagram It: Compound Adjectives (T)
STEP 5 **Listening and Reading Comprehension** • Use context-based strategies to define words. • Identify signal words for comprehension: **distinguish, select**. • Identify main ideas.	❑ Exercise 5: Phrase It ❑ Independent Text: "Extreme Athletes" ❑ Exercise 6: Use the Clues	❑ Passage Fluency 2
STEP 6 **Speaking and Writing** • Organize main ideas for writing. • Apply outline to writing an introductory paragraph.	❑ Exercise 7: Rewrite It: Pronouns	❑ Exercise 8: Rewrite It: Pronouns
Self-Evaluation (5 is the highest) **Effort** = I produced my best work. **Participation** = I was actively involved in tasks. **Independence** = I worked on my own.	**Effort:** 1 2 3 4 5 **Participation:** 1 2 3 4 5 **Independence:** 1 2 3 4 5	**Effort:** 1 2 3 4 5 **Participation:** 1 2 3 4 5 **Independence:** 1 2 3 4 5
Teacher Evaluation	**Effort:** 1 2 3 4 5 **Participation:** 1 2 3 4 5 **Independence:** 1 2 3 4 5	**Effort:** 1 2 3 4 5 **Participation:** 1 2 3 4 5 **Independence:** 1 2 3 4 5

Lesson 8 (Date:_____)	**Lesson 9** (Date:_____)	**Lesson 10** (Date:_____)
❑ Exercise 1: Listening for Word Parts	❑ Exercise 1: Listening for Stressed Syllables	❑ Exercise 1: Listening for Stressed Syllables
❑ Drop It (T) ❑ Word Fluency 4	❑ Exercise 2: Build It	❑ Content Mastery: Spelling Posttest 2
❑ Content Mastery: Word Relationships ❑ Content Mastery: Morphology	❑ Exercise 3: Find It: Present and Past Participles as Adjectives ❑ Expression of the Day	❑ Exercise 2: Sort It ❑ Draw It: Idioms ❑ Expression of the Day
❑ Masterpiece Sentences: All Stages ❑ Rewrite It: Compound Adjective	❑ Exercise 4: Find It: Object of the Preposition ❑ Exercise 5: Find It: Compound Adjectives	❑ Content Mastery: Plural and Possessive Nouns, Prepositional Phrases, and Compound Adjectives
❑ Instructional Text: "Tony Hawk: Extreme Athlete" ❑ Exercise 2: Use the Clues	❑ Exercise 6: Blueprint for Reading: Identifying Main Ideas (T)	❑ Exercise 6: Blueprint for Reading: Identifying Main Ideas (T) (Lesson 9)
❑ Exercise 3: Answer It	❑ Exercise 7: Blueprint for Writing: Outline (T) ❑ Exercise 8: Paraphrase It: Sentences for an Introductory Paragraph ❑ Challenge Text: "Roberto Clemente: The Heart of the Diamond"	❑ Exercise 7: Blueprint for Writing: Outline (T) (Lesson 9) ❑ Exercise 3: Paraphrase It ❑ Exercise 4: Write It ❑ Challenge Text: "Roberto Clemente: The Heart of the Diamond"
Effort: 1 2 3 4 5 **Participation:** 1 2 3 4 5 **Independence:** 1 2 3 4 5	**Effort:** 1 2 3 4 5 **Participation:** 1 2 3 4 5 **Independence:** 1 2 3 4 5	**Effort:** 1 2 3 4 5 **Participation:** 1 2 3 4 5 **Independence:** 1 2 3 4 5
Effort: 1 2 3 4 5 **Participation:** 1 2 3 4 5 **Independence:** 1 2 3 4 5	**Effort:** 1 2 3 4 5 **Participation:** 1 2 3 4 5 **Independence:** 1 2 3 4 5	**Effort:** 1 2 3 4 5 **Participation:** 1 2 3 4 5 **Independence:** 1 2 3 4 5

Exercise 1 · Spelling Pretest 1

▸ Write each word your teacher repeats.

1. _____   6. _____   11. _____

2. _____   7. _____   12. _____

3. _____   8. _____   13. _____

4. _____   9. _____   14. _____

5. _____   10. _____   15. _____

Exercise 2 · Identify It: Plural or Possessive

▸ Read each sentence.

▸ Decide if the underlined word is a plural noun, a singular possessive noun, or a plural possessive noun.

▸ Fill in the correct bubble.

	Plural Noun	Singular Possessive	Plural Possessive
1. <u>Steven's</u> desire to win was impressive.	◯	◯	◯
2. Many different events test the <u>athletes'</u> skills.	◯	◯	◯
3. The Special <u>Olympics'</u> motto is inspiring.	◯	◯	◯
4. There are <u>medals</u> for all who take part.	◯	◯	◯
5. <u>Everyone's</u> effort is amazing.	◯	◯	◯

Exercise 3 · Find It: Possessives—Pronouns and Adjectives

▸ Read each sentence.

▸ Circle the possessive pronoun or adjective in each sentence.

▸ Write P for the possessive pronoun or A for the possessive adjective on the line.

1. Special Olympians from our state took part in the games. _____

2. We thought the best team was ours. _____

3. Mark and his brother loved living in the athlete's dorm. _____

4. This clothing must be yours. _____

5. The boy said the medal was his. _____

6. She and her friends did this as volunteers. _____

7. His main event was swimming the backstroke. _____

8. The team won its first game easily. _____

9. That uniform is mine. _____

10. Your donation to Special Olympics will be added to theirs. _____

Unit 16 · Lesson 1

Exercise 4 · Phrase It

▸ Read the sentences as you would speak them.

▸ Use the penciling strategy to "scoop" the phrases in each sentence.

▸ The first two are done for you as examples.

1. One person can make things happen.

2. Shriver began a summer day camp.

3. The camp was for athletes.

4. She held the camp at her home.

5. She invited kids like Steven.

6. She watched them compete in sports.

7. Shriver saw them smile.

8. Athletes come to play in the games.

9. These athletes compete at no cost.

10. Help fund Special Olympics!

Exercise 1 · Listening for Sounds in Words

▸ Listen to each word your teacher says.

▸ Decide where the long vowel sound occurs in the word.

▸ Circle the position of the long vowel sound:
B for beginning, **M** for middle, and **E** for end.

1. B   M   E

2. B   M   E

3. B   M   E

4. B   M   E

5. B   M   E

6. B   M   E

7. B   M   E

8. B   M   E

9. B   M   E

10. B   M   E

Exercise 2 · Sort It: Syllable Types

▸ Read the words in the **Word Bank**.

▸ Sort the words according to their syllable type.

▸ Write each word under the correct heading.

Word Bank

fine	ate	she	came
back	side	pass	we
be	fig	hand	he

closed	final silent -e	open

Exercise 3 · Find It: Past Participles

▸ Each sentence contains a past participle ending in **-ed** or **-en**.

▸ Read each sentence.

▸ Underline the past participle and the noun that it describes or modifies.

▸ Answer the question about the noun.

▸ Use the examples as models.

Part A

Sentence	What kind? or Which one?
Example: <u>Broken glass</u> fell from the ornate frame.	What kind of glass? **broken**
Example: The undercover cops observe the <u>deserted apartment</u>.	What kind of apartment? **deserted**
1. Chen will ask the uninvited visitors to depart.	Which visitors?
2. Shattered glass ruined the front tires of Pedro's car.	What kind of glass?
3. The pampered child whined all day.	Which child?
4. Lu and Chen discover the misfiled papers just in time for class.	What papers?
5. Before the game, Ramon was named the designated hitter.	What kind of hitter?

(continued)

Unit 16 · Lesson 2

Exercise 3 (continued) · Find It: Past Participles

Part B

Use the underlined past participles from **Part A** to complete the activities.

6. Complete the antonym pair:

   invited: _____

7. Complete the synonym pair:

   spoiled: _____

8. Complete this sentence.

   The runners get water at _____ spots along the race route.

9. Define the word **misfile:**

   _____

10. Choose two of the part participles you underlined and use them in sentences.
    Make sure the past participle in each sentence does the job of an adjective.

    _____

    _____

Exercise 4 · Find It: Prepositional Phrases

▸ Read each sentence.

▸ Find and underline each prepositional phrase.

▸ Circle the preposition.

1. Mrs. Shriver began the camp in 1963.

2. The campers worked hard at many sports.

3. After many drills, the campers became better athletes.

4. The athletes displayed great pride in their talents.

5. Today, campers with limited skills compete around the world.

Exercise 5 · Identify It: Object of the Preposition

▸ Read each sentence.

▸ Decide if the underlined noun in each sentence functions as a direct object or as an object of a preposition.

▸ Fill in the bubble to mark the answer.

	Direct Object	Object of Preposition
1. Mark had many <u>problems</u> with skills.	◯	◯
2. He needed extra help with his <u>skills</u>.	◯	◯
3. Special Olympics are important for many <u>people</u>.	◯	◯
4. They have become an international <u>event</u>.	◯	◯
5. The athletes compete at no <u>cost</u>.	◯	◯

Unit 16 · Lesson 2

Exercise 6 · Find It: Words With Final Silent -e

▶ Read the excerpt from **"The Complete Athlete."**

▶ Highlight or underline words with final silent -**e**.

▶ Sort the words according to their long vowel sound.

---

from "The Complete Athlete"

Now, Special Olympics is important in the lives of many people. Today, there are 26 sports. There are summer and winter sports. From all over the world, athletes come to play in the games. These athletes compete at no cost. How are the games funded? Shriver has used grants. Many have donated. Many others have made money with events. You can help, too. Get started! Help fund Special Olympics!

$\bar{a}$	$\bar{e}$	$\bar{\imath}$	$\bar{o}$	$\overline{oo}$

Exercise 7 · Use the Clues

▶ Read the sentence pairs.

▶ Read the pronoun that is circled.

▶ Identify the noun that the pronoun replaces in each sentence.

▶ Draw an arrow to show the link between the pronoun and the noun it replaces.

▶ Underline the noun that was replaced by the pronoun.

1. Mark loves sports. (He) is not like other athletes.

2. There are many like Mark and Kate. Yes, (their) skills are limited.

3. Shriver began a summer day camp. (She) held the camp at her home.

4. She invited kids like Mark and Kate. She watched (them) compete in sports.

5. From all over the world, athletes come to play in the games. (They) compete at no cost.

Exercise 8 · Rewrite It: Pronouns

▶ Reread each pair of sentences in Exercise 7, **Use the Clues**.

▶ Replace the pronoun with the noun that it represents.

▶ Rewrite the sentence using the noun.

▶ Read the new sentence.

▶ Check for sentence signals—capital letters, commas, and end punctuation.

1. _____

2. _____

3. _____

4. _____

5. _____

Exercise 1 · Listening for Sounds in Words

▶ Listen to each word your teacher says.

▶ Put an X in the column to indicate the long vowel sound you hear.

	$\bar{a}$	$\bar{e}$	$\bar{i}$	$\bar{o}$	$\overline{oo}$
1.					
2.					
3.					
4.					
5.					
6.					
7.					
8.					
9.					
10.					

Exercise 2 · Divide It

▸ Read the sentence silently.

▸ Use the steps of **Divide It** to break the **boldface** words into syllables.

▸ Blend the syllables together to read each boldface word.

▸ After dividing, read the sentences to a partner.

▸ Follow along with your teacher's example to complete the first item.

1. The **athletes compete** in the track events.

   athletes   compete

2. A **finite** set of games **protect** the purpose of the Olympics.

   finite   protect

3. All **competitors** are **honored** whether they win or not.

   competitors   honored

Exercise 3 · Find It: Essential Words

▸ Find the **Essential Words** for this unit in these sentences.

▸ Underline them. There may be more than one in a sentence.

1. Tomorrow, we are going to compete again.

2. Today is Special Olympics!

3. I want to be brave in the attempt to win.

4. I will work hard and do my best.

5. Run when you hear the sound of the bell.

▸ Write the **Essential Words** in the spaces.

_____   _____   _____

_____   _____   _____

Exercise 4 · Define It

▸ Fill in the blanks with a category and an attribute to define the word.

▸ Compare definitions that you're unsure of with a dictionary definition.

▸ Do the first word with your teacher.

1. An **athlete** is a(n) _____ who _____

_____

_____ .

2. **Brave** is a(n) _____ that _____

_____

_____ .

3. A **game** is a(n) _____ that _____

_____

_____ .

4. A **backbone** is a(n) _____ that _____

_____

_____ .

5. **Compete** is a(n) _____ that _____

_____

_____ .

6. A **candidate** is a(n) _____ who _____

_____

_____ .

7. A **hurricane** is a(n) _____ that _____

_____

_____ .

(continued)

Exercise 4 (continued) · Define It

8. **Climate** is a(n) _____ that _____

_____

_____.

9. A **trombone** is a(n) _____ that _____

_____

_____.

10. A **minute** is a(n) _____ that _____

_____

_____.

Which vocabulary words are related to **athletes**?

▸ Write the words in the blanks.

_____   _____   _____

_____   _____   _____

Unit 16 · Lesson 3

Exercise 5 · Identify It: Main Verb or Helping Verb

▸ Read each sentence with your teacher.

▸ Underline the verb or verb phrase in each sentence.

▸ Decide if the form of the verb **be** or **have** is used as a main verb or a helping verb.

▸ Do the first sentence with your teacher.

	Main Verb	Helping Verb
1. The athlete has waited an hour.	○	○
2. We were prepared for the long and hot game.	○	○
3. She is our strong and energetic team leader.	○	○
4. Our team has scored many difficult points.	○	○
5. At last, we were victorious.	○	○
6. There will be an extreme sports competition this winter.	○	○
7. Next year we will enter a well-trained and competitive team.	○	○
8. Mark has tried many different sports.	○	○
9. The scoreboard was flashing the winning time.	○	○
10. Mark has four gold medals.	○	○

Exercise 6 · Use the Clues

▶ Use context clues to define the word **divisions**.

▶ Underline the vocabulary word.

▶ Read the text surrounding the unknown word.

▶ Circle the meaning signal.

▶ Underline the word that helps define the unknown word.

---

from "A Special Kind of Athlete"

Special Olympics is organized with fairness in mind. People of about the same age and ability compete in divisions. Team sports have three age divisions, or groups. This helps participants with more than physical development. It helps their self-esteem. It boosts self-confidence. Everyone has a chance to win.

▶ Write a definition based on the context clues.

▶ Verify your definition with the dictionary or www.yourdictionary.com.

divisions – _____

Exercise 7 · Answer It

▸ Underline the signal word in the question.

▸ Write the answer in complete sentences.

1. Distinguish Special Olympics from the Olympic Games.

Special Olympics	Olympic Games

2. What can you infer about the message in the Special Olympics Athlete Oath (lines 10–11)?

_____

_____

_____

(continued)

Exercise 7 *(continued)* · **Answer It**

3. Select four examples of events included in Special Olympics. Select three additional events that could be included in Special Olympics.

   _____

   _____

   _____

   _____

   _____

4. Distinguish whether the following statements about Special Olympics are facts or opinions.

   a) Special Olympics began as a day camp.   _____

   b) Special Olympics is a great event.   _____

   c) Today Special Olympics has 26 official sports.   _____

   d) Special Olympics athletes are determined.   _____

   e) Special Olympics is different from the Olympic Games.   _____

5. What can you infer about Steven Walker's personality?

   _____

   _____

   _____

Exercise 1 · Syllable Awareness: Segmentation

▸ Listen to the word your teacher says.

▸ Count the syllables in each word. Write the number in the first column.

▸ Write the letter for each vowel sound you hear in the word.

▸ Mark each vowel with the correct diacritical mark.

- Short vowel sound with a breve (˘).

- Long vowel sound with a macron (ˉ).

- **r**-controlled vowel sound, the vowel before the **r** with a circumflex (ˆ).

	How many syllables do you hear?	First vowel sound	Second vowel sound	Third vowel sound
1.				
2.				
3.				
4.				
5.				
6.				
7.				
8.				
9.				
10.				

Exercise 2 · Build It: Prefixed Words

▸ Read the prefixes and syllables in the **Word Bank**.

▸ Combine the prefix **sub-** with the syllables in the **Word Bank** to make new words.

▸ Record the words on the line under the correct heading.

▸ Check a dictionary to verify that words are real words.

Word Bank

sub-		set	urb
plot	ject	mit	tract

sub-

_____   _____

_____   _____

_____   _____

▸ Read the words that you built with the prefix **sub-**. You can add **-ed** to three of them. Write them here:

_____   _____   _____

Unit 16 · Lesson 4

Exercise 3 · Define It: Prefixed Words

▶ Record the meaning of the prefix **sub-**.

▶ Use the definition of **sub-** to fill in the blanks.

▶ Verify your definition with a dictionary.

1. The prefix **sub-** means _____.

2. **Subsoil** means the soil that is _____.

3. A **subtotal** is a total _____.

4. **Way** is an old word for **road**. A **subway** travels _____.

5. One meaning of **marine** is *sea or ocean*.

   A **submarine** travels _____.

Exercise 4 · Identify It: Suffixes -ed and -en

▸ Each sentence contains one word ending in **-ed** or **-en**.

▸ In some of these words **-ed** and **-en** are suffixes.

▸ In some of the words the letters <u>ed</u> and <u>en</u> are not suffixes; they are just part of the word.

▸ Underline the words that end with **-ed** or **-en**.

▸ Do the examples with your teacher. Check the appropriate column.

Sentence	Verb Suffix	Adjective Suffix	Not a suffix
Example: Nina's classmates <u>picked</u> up all the trash in the park after the rally.	X		
Example: The <u>perplexed</u> students wandered in and out of the empty school.		X	
Example: The <u>firemen</u> rush to the fire and put out the flames.			X
1. Clint tossed the antifreeze container into Chan's trunk.			
2. The teacher had over a hundred reports on his desk.			
3. The confused student got on the wrong bus after the class trip.			
4. Carlos composed music for a film about skating.			
5. My amused classmates voted on the best act.			

Unit 16 · Lesson 4

Exercise 5 · Rewrite It: Irregular Verb Forms

▸ Read the sentences.

▸ Underline the verbs in each sentence.

▸ Rewrite the sentences, changing the verbs to the past tense.

▸ Use the irregular past tense verbs in the chart in your *Student Text*.

1. The athletes overcome problems to compete.

_____

2. One boy overtakes a runner and wins the race.

_____

3. Another becomes a superstar overnight.

_____

4. The supporters sell tickets and make money for their team.

_____

_____

5. A player mistakes one brother for another.

_____

Exercise 6 · Find It: Irregular Past Tense

▸ Read the text adapted from "**The Complete Athlete**."

▸ Find all the irregular past tense verbs and underline them.

Note: There are ten irregular verbs.

---

based on "The Complete Athlete"

Shriver thought about campers with limited skills. She began a summer day camp for them. The camp was for athletes. She held the camp at her home. Then she brought in trainers to help the campers learn sports. The athletes were thrilled. They gave their best effort. Some became very good at different sports. All the contestants who took part in the events won medals.

Exercise 7 · Blueprint for Reading: Identifying Main Ideas

▸ Highlight the main ideas in blue.

from "A Special Kind of Athlete"

Special Olympics is a unique sporting event. What's different about it? All the athletes have intellectual disabilities. The coaches are volunteers. The trainers are volunteers. Even the officials are volunteers. Special Olympics achieves three goals. The games provide experience. They boost self-confidence. They give the athletes the joy of competition. Ability is not the focus. Every athlete gets the positive experience of competing in a sport. In fact, the Special Olympics Athlete Oath reads: "Let me win. But if I cannot, let me be brave in the attempt."

Special Olympics has grown over the years. It began as a day camp. It grew rapidly. It became an international event. The first International Special Olympics Games began in 1968. Chicago was the first host. It was a huge success. Many communities began to host games. Today, the games have 26 official sports. There are individual events like gymnastics and swimming. There are team sports like basketball and softball. More than a million athletes participate. They come from all around the world. There are more than 500,000 volunteers.

The athletes' families play a key role in Special Olympics. Board chair Sargent Shriver explained, "Families are the backbone of Special Olympics. They help to coach and train their athletes. They

(continued)

provide transportation. They sit on the board of directors. They raise money."

George Ashley was a coach. He was there for his stepdaughter, Shannon. Ashley learned that everybody wins. He is an amateur athlete himself. He said Special Olympics taught him the true meaning of sport. "It was really the most rewarding thing I have ever done," he said. "I went into it thinking I was this big, tough guy. I found out that there are many things we take for granted. To be at the finish line when a competitor comes in and see the sense of accomplishment is worth whatever work goes into it. I think anyone who plays a sport should take some time and volunteer for Special Olympics."

Special Olympics is organized with fairness in mind. People compete in divisions. Each division has competitors of about the same age and ability. Team sports have three age divisions. This helps participants with more than physical development. It helps their self-esteem. It boosts self-confidence. Everyone has a chance to win.

Special Olympics is different from the Olympic Games. In the Olympic Games, much time, money, and effort are invested in winning. The number of gold medals won is very important. In contrast, Special Olympics places more importance on participation. Winning is not as important. All competitors are honored whether they win or not.

Exercise 8 · Blueprint for Writing: Outline

_____

I. _____

II. _____

III. _____

IV. _____

_____

Exercise 9 · Paraphrase It: Sentences for an Introductory Paragraph

▸ Paraphrase the first two main ideas on the **Blueprint for Writing: Outline**.

▸ Record them here.

I. _____

_____

II. _____

_____

Exercise 1 · Word Networks: Antonyms, Synonyms, and Attributes

▸ Read each word pair.

▸ Sort the word pairs according to their relationship.

▸ Discuss your answers with a partner.

admire: respect	arrive: depart	hurricane: wind	secure: safe
parade: drum	provide: give	complete: begin	polite: rude
math: divide	include: exclude	create: make	band: trombone

Antonyms (opposite)	Synonyms (same)	Attributes

Exercise 2 · Paraphrase It: Sentences for an Introductory Paragraph

▸ Paraphrase the last two main ideas on the **Blueprint for Writing: Outline**.

▸ Record them here.

III. _____

_____

IV. _____

_____

Exercise 3 · Write It: Introductory Paragraph for a Multiparagraph Composition

▸ Write the introductory paragraph.

▸ Read the entire multiparagraph composition with your teacher.

_____

_____

_____

_____

_____

_____

_____

(continued)

Special Olympics has increased since its beginnings. It has grown from a day camp to an international event. Today, there are 26 official sports in Special Olympics. More than a million athletes come from all over the world to compete in the event. Over 500,000 volunteers assist in Special Olympics.

Families have many important functions in Special Olympics. They participate in the coaching and training of participants. Families help with transportation. They also hold positions on the board of directors. Finally, families work hard to collect money for Special Olympics.

Fairness plays a key role in the organization of Special Olympics. Divisions consist of similar ages and ability levels. This helps to build both physical skills and self-confidence. All athletes have the opportunity to win.

Special Olympics is not like the Olympic Games. In the Olympic Games, enormous amounts of time, money, and effort are spent in the pursuit of winning. Countries try to collect the most gold medals. Special Olympics has different goals. Participation is more important than winning. All Special Olympics athletes are celebrated for their efforts.

Special Olympics has provided a positive experience for countless athletes with disabilities. Over the years the event has grown tremendously. The support of athletes' families has proven beneficial to the growth and success of this event. The goal of guaranteeing fairness for all athletes sets Special Olympics apart from other international sporting competitions. Special Olympics is truly an amazing event.

Exercise 1 · Listening for Stressed Syllables

▸ Listen to each word your teacher says. Repeat the word.

▸ Listen for the stressed syllable.

▸ Make an X in the box to mark the position of the stressed syllable.

▸ Listen for schwa in the unstressed syllable. Highlight or circle the vowel when it is reduced to schwa.

Word	1st Syllable	2nd Syllable
1. comprise		
2. invoke		
3. transcribe		
4. purchase		
5. escape		

Exercise 2 · Spelling Pretest 2

▸ Listen to the word your teacher repeats.

▸ Write the word.

1. _____
2. _____
3. _____
4. _____
5. _____

6. _____
7. _____
8. _____
9. _____
10. _____

11. _____
12. _____
13. _____
14. _____
15. _____

Exercise 3 · Word Networks: Analogies

▸ Read the first word pair.

▸ Underline the word that names the relationship: **synonym, antonym, attribute**.

▸ Choose a word from the **Word Bank** that has the same relationship to the word in the second part of the analogy.

▸ Write the word in the blank to complete the analogy.

▸ Discuss your answers with a partner.

Word Bank

wind	safe	make
begin	divide	exclude

1. provide : give :: create: Relationship: synonym   antonym   attribute

     _____

2. polite : rude :: complete: Relationship: synonym   antonym   attribute

     _____

3. admire : respect :: secure: Relationship: synonym   antonym   attribute

     _____

4. arrive : depart :: include: Relationship: synonym   antonym   attribute

     _____

5. storm : thunder :: hurricane: Relationship: synonym   antonym   attribute

     _____

Exercise 4 · Find It: Compound Adjectives

▸ Read each sentence.

▸ Underline the compound adjective.

▸ Circle the conjunction that joins the compound adjective.

▸ Draw an arrow to the noun it describes.

1. Worldwide and international events are held in different places.

2. Challenging or exciting events sold out quickly.

3. Committed and dedicated athletes attend the Special Olympics.

4. The team could wear red or black sneakers.

5. When athletes finish a race, they feel happy and satisfied.

6. Extreme sports involve risky and daring tricks.

7. Strong but light helmets protect skaters' heads.

8. Abrupt and quick stops can injure the skaters.

9. Skaters have developed a new and interesting jargon.

10. The new jargon is difficult and hard for others to understand.

Exercise 5 · Phrase It

▸ Using the penciling strategy to "scoop" the phrases in each sentence.

▸ Read the sentence as you would speak it.

▸ The first two are done for you .

1. Extreme athletes love risks.

2. Extreme skaters are fine athletes.

3. Inline skates are not like skates of the past.

4. They are light, fast, and strong.

5. Skaters use their own jargon.

6. Bashing means going down steps.

7. They take their skating to the next level!

8. Extreme sports have added risks.

9. Without protection, skaters get hurt.

10. Safe athletes wear helmets and use pads.

Unit 16 · Lesson 6

Exercise 6 · Use the Clues

▸ Read the sentence pairs.

▸ Read the pronoun that is circled.

▸ Identify the noun that the pronoun replaces in each sentence.

▸ Draw an arrow to show the link between the pronoun and the noun it replaces.

▸ Underline the noun replaced by the pronoun.

1. Extreme athletes love risks. (They) do their sport and add a twist.

2. Extreme skaters use inline skates. (They)'re not like the skates of the past.

3. Extreme skaters use inline skates. (They) don't use skating rinks.

4. Take the top of the ramp. (It) has a name.

5. Safe athletes protect themselves. (They) use helmets and pads.

Unit 16 · Lesson 6

Exercise 7 · Rewrite It: Pronouns

▶ Reread each pair of sentences in Exercise 6, **Use the Clues**.

▶ Replace the pronoun with the noun or noun phrase that it represents.

▶ Rewrite the sentence using the noun.

▶ Read the new sentence.

▶ Check for sentence signals—capital letters and end punctuation.

▶ Do the first one with your teacher.

1. _____

2. _____

3. _____

4. _____

5. _____

Exercise 1 · Listening for Word Parts

▶ Listen to each word your teacher says.

▶ Mark **Yes** if you hear a suffix or **No** if you don't hear a suffix.

▶ If you hear a suffix, write the suffix you hear.

	Do you hear a suffix on the word?		If **Yes**, what is the suffix?
	Yes	No	
1.			
2.			
3.			
4.			
5.			
6.			
7.			
8.			
9.			
10.			

Exercise 2 · Listening for Stressed Syllables

▶ Listen to each word your teacher says. Repeat the word.

▶ Listen for the stressed syllable.

▶ Make an X in the box to mark the position of the stressed syllable.

▶ Listen for schwa in the unstressed syllable. Highlight or circle the vowel when it is reduced to schwa.

Word	1st Syllable	2nd Syllable	3rd Syllable
1. positive			
2. arrive			
3. exclude			
4. oppose			
5. tribute			

Exercise 3 · Divide It

▸ Read the sentence silently.

▸ Use the steps of **Divide It** to break the **boldfaced** words into syllables.

▸ Blend the syllables together to read each boldfaced word.

▸ After dividing, read the sentences to a partner.

▸ Follow along with your teacher's example to complete the first item.

1. He was **determined** to **accomplish athletic** feats.

   determined   accomplish   athletic

2. Tony has a six-**figure contract**.

   figure   contract

3. **Extreme** skaters **refine** their skills.

   extreme   refine

4. Skaters use **helmets** so that they don't get **injured**.

   helmets   injured

Exercise 4 · Find It: Contractions

▸ Read the sentences.

▸ Circle the contractions.

▸ Expand each contraction into two words on the lines below.

1. They'd offered him a big bonus.

2. She's been using her helmet.

3. You'd better not get injured!

4. It's been a huge accomplishment.

5. He's defined the rules at work.

1. _____

2. _____

3. _____

4. _____

5. _____

Exercise 5 · Define It

▸ Record the meaning of the prefix **anti-**.

▸ Use the definition of **anti-** to complete each sentence.

▸ Check your answers in a dictionary.

1. The prefix **anti-** means _____.

2. **Antiwar** means _____.

3. **Septic** means *germs* or *filth*. An **antiseptic** works _____.

4. The **antihero's** personality is _____ from that of a hero.

5. **Antifreeze** in a car's radiator protects it _____.

Unit 16 · Lesson 7

Exercise 6 · Find It: Past Participle Phrases

▸ Read each sentence.

▸ Look at the underlined noun.

▸ Copy the adjective and past participle phrase that describe each noun.

▸ Work through the first two examples with your teacher.

Sentence	*What kind?* or *Which one?*
Example: The athletic <u>girls</u>, dressed in team uniforms, took part in the track meet.	What kind of girls? a. _____ b. _____
Example: The angry <u>chicken</u>, covered in mud, clucked loudly.	What kind of chicken? a. _____ b. _____
1. The loud <u>band</u>, hired by Brad, played all night for his party.	Which band? a. _____ b. _____
2. The daring <u>divers</u>, protected by antishark cages, explored the sea floor.	Which divers? a. _____ b. _____
3. Prepared for the test, the successful <u>student</u> passed with high marks.	Which student? a. _____ b. _____
4. The old <u>soldier</u>, decorated with medals, stood at attention.	Which soldier? a. _____ b. _____

(continued)

Exercise 6 (continued) · Find It: Past Participle Phrases

Sentence	*What kind?* or *Which one?*
5. The unhappy dog, enclosed in the yard, barked all night.	Which dog? a. _____ b. _____

Exercise 7 · Diagram It: Compound Adjectives

▸ Read each sentence.

▸ Do the first diagram with your teacher.

▸ Make an **X** above the vertical line that separates the complete subject from the complete predicate.

▸ Diagram the remaining sentences on your own.

▸ Review your diagrams and make necessary corrections.

1. Tired but proud runners accepted their medals.

2. Extreme skaters do risky and daring tricks.

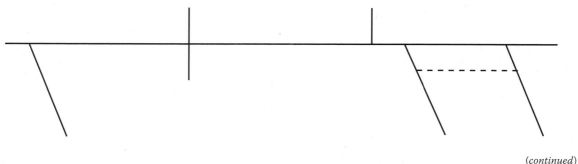

(*continued*)

Exercise 7 (continued) · Diagram It: Compound Adjectives

3. Young and old daredevils try extreme sports.

4. Extreme sports capture the vivid and active imaginations of young people.

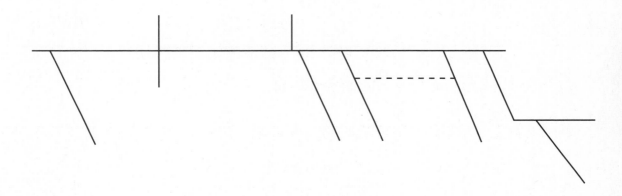

5. Skateboarders live risky but exciting lives.

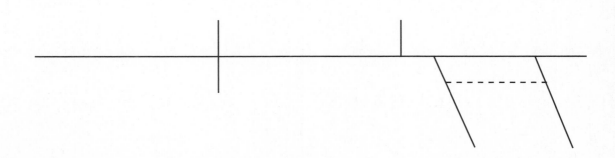

Unit 16 · Lesson 7

Exercise 8 · Rewrite It: Pronouns

▸ Read each sentence.

▸ Replace the underlined pronoun with a word or phrase that means the same as **extreme athletes**.

▸ Rewrite the sentence.

▸ Read your new sentence.

1. <u>They</u> love the risk.

   _____

2. <u>They</u> don't use skating rinks.

   _____

3. <u>They</u> use steps and even curbs.

   _____

4. <u>They</u> spend lots of time practicing.

   _____

5. <u>They</u> take their sport to a new level.

   _____

Exercise 1 · Listening for Word Parts

▸ Listen to each word your teacher says.

▸ Mark **Yes** or **No** to show whether the word has a suffix.

▸ If **Yes**, write the suffix.

	Do you hear a suffix on the word?		If **Yes**, what is the suffix?
	Yes	**No**	
1.			
2.			
3.			
4.			
5.			
6.			
7.			
8.			
9.			
10.			

Exercise 2 · Use the Clues

▸ Use meaning signals to define **retired**.

▸ Put a box around the vocabulary word.

▸ Read the text surrounding the unknown word.

▸ Circle the meaning signals.

▸ Underline the words that help define the unknown word.

---

from "Tony Hawk: Extreme Athlete"

Tony retired from professional skateboarding when he was 35. But in skateboarding, the word "retire" doesn't mean he stopped skating. It just means he's stopped competitive skating. He still skates almost every day. He learns new tricks. He does several public demonstrations a year.

▸ Write a definition based on the context clues.

▸ Verify your definition with the dictionary or www.yourdictionary.com.

_____

_____

Exercise 3 · Answer It

▶ Underline the signal word in each sentence.

▶ Answer each question in a complete sentence.

▶ Underline the part of the sentence that answers the question.

1. Select examples that illustrate how Tony Hawk is an extreme athlete.

_____

_____

_____

_____

_____

_____

_____

_____

2. Tony Hawk was hard on himself as a child. Tell about the experience of someone you know who was trying to learn a sport.

_____

_____

_____

_____

_____

_____

_____

_____

(continued)

3. Lines 10–11 state, "Tony started playing on the bright blue board. Crash! Bang! Slam!" The words **crash**, **bang**, and **slam** are examples of onomatopoeia. Explain the effect this type of word has on the reader.

_____

_____

_____

_____

_____

4. List Hawk's accomplishments.

_____

_____

_____

_____

_____

_____

_____

_____

_____

_____

_____

_____

(continued)

Exercise 3 (continued) · Answer It

5. The sport of skateboarding and Tony Hawk's career declined but later became successful again. The author describes Hawk's rising success with the statement, "And the Hawk became the 'Phoenix'." Explain what the author meant by this statement.

_____

_____

_____

_____

_____

_____

_____

_____

Exercise 1 · Listening for Stressed Syllables

▸ Listen to each word your teacher says. Repeat the word.

▸ Listen for the stressed syllable.

▸ Make an X in the box to mark the position of the stressed syllable.

▸ Listen for schwa in the unstressed syllable. Highlight or circle the vowel when it is reduced to schwa.

Word	1st Syllable	2nd Syllable	3rd Syllable
1. prescribe			
2. permissive			
3. decline			
4. require			
5. elope			

Exercise 2 · Build It

▸ Combine prefixes and suffixes in the middle square with base words.

Example: sub + divide +ed = subdivided

▸ Record words in the chart below according to the headings.

▸ Use the **Drop e** spelling rule when necessary.

▸ Use a dictionary to verify that you are building real words.

▸ Add any new words that you find.

divide	scribe	mistake
forgive	sub- -ed anti- -en	septic
theft	lock	compact

(continued)

Exercise 2 (continued) · Build It

sub-	anti-	other

Exercise 3 · Find It: Past and Present Participles as Adjectives

▸ Each sentence contains a present or past participle that is used as an adjective.

▸ Underline the participles and copy them into the appropriate column.

▸ Other words in the sentences may end with the letters **-ing**, **-ed**, or **-en**. If they are not adjectives, do not include them.

▸ Work through the examples with your teacher.

(continued)

Exercise 3 (continued) · Find It: Past and Present Participles as Adjectives

Sentence	Present Participle Job: adjective that describes what the noun is doing.	Past Participle Job: adjective that usually describes what was done by or happened to the noun.
Examples: It is hard to kick a deflated football.		
The skidding car crashed into the telephone pole.		
Broken glass littered the side walk.		
1. After their walk, the tired hikers rested on their packs.		
2. Prepared for his final exam, Ted arrived at school that morning with a positive attitude.		
3. The diving champ won a gold medal at the Olympic Games.		
4. The ice on the frozen pond was thick enough for skating.		
5. He read about the exploding flashcube trick in a novel.		
6. The broken posts could not support the huge pile of wood.		
7. The converted sedan became a great race car.		
8. The raging winds tore trees out of the ground.		
9. Bothered by injury, the athlete could not compete.		
10. The developing news story preempted the local news.		

Unit 16 · Lesson 9

Exercise 4 · Find It: Object of the Preposition

▸ Read the text.

▸ Find and underline the prepositional phrases.

▸ Circle the object of each preposition.

based on "Extreme Athlete"

Some young and eager athletes love to take risks in their chosen sports. They get a thrill from the daring skills. Beginners start with small and simple tricks. Then they spend lots of time practicing these. When they are good at the small tricks, they add harder and more difficult ones. Inline skaters are a good example of extreme athletes. They use skates with light and strong wheels. They skate in parks, and on the sidewalks. Passersby often stop and admire the skills of these amazing and daring athletes.

Exercise 5 · Find It: Compound Adjectives

▶ Reread the text from Exercise 4, **Find It: Object of the Preposition**.

▶ Find and copy the compound adjectives and the nouns they modify onto the lines below.

Hint: There are five compound adjectives.

1. _____

2. _____

3. _____

4. _____

5. _____

Exercise 6 · Blueprint for Reading: Identifying Main Ideas

▸ Highlight the main ideas in blue.

based on "Tony Hawk: Extreme Athlete"

Tony Hawk began skateboarding as a child. By 12, Tony was sponsored by a skateboard company. By 14, he was pro. By 16, Tony was the best skateboarder in the world. Over the next 17 years, he entered about 100 contests. He won 73 and placed second in 19. His record is by far the best in skateboarding history.

Tony had great financial success early in his career. For example, he was able to buy his own house when he was a 17-year-old high school senior. Two years later, he bought another house. This time, Tony built a monster skate ramp at the top of a hill. He wedged a smaller ramp between his house and pool. In addition, Tony traveled worldwide for demonstrations and contests. He made enough money to buy trips to Hawaii for his friends. Everyone could vacation together. In addition, Tony was an electronics nut. He was always updating his computers, stereo systems, video cameras, and cars.

(continued)

Exercise 6 (continued) · Blueprint for Reading: Identifying Main Ideas

This financial success did not last forever. In 1991, it all came to an end. People lost interest in skateboarding. Skating died. As a result, Tony's income shrank drastically. During this time, Tony lived in a blur of financial uncertainty. He sold one house. He refinanced the other. He started a skateboard company with a fellow skateboarder. The company didn't make money. Tony's future was unclear. "I thought skating was over for me," he said. He realized that he might not be able to earn a living skating. He thought of options. He could edit video. He could get a computer job.

Tony's success rose again. Skateboarding came back. His company began to succeed. It is now one of the largest skateboarding companies in the world. In addition, Tony signed six-figure endorsement deals. In 1999 Tony hooked up with an electronics company. Together, they created a skateboarding video game. It became a best seller. Tony's success overflowed into the non-athletic world as well. His autobiography, *HAWK—Occupation: Skateboarder* was a *New York Times* best seller. A final example of Tony's success is the Tony Hawk Foundation. It promotes and helps finance public skate parks in low-income neighborhoods across America. Tony feels that it is important to give back to the sport that has given him so much. Now in retirement, Tony continues to enjoy his extreme sport.

Exercise 7 · Blueprint for Writing: Outline

_____

I. _____

II. _____

III. _____

IV. _____

_____

Exercise 8 · Paraphrase It: Sentences for an Introductory Paragraph

▸ Paraphrase the first two main ideas on the **Blueprint for Writing: Outline**.

▸ Record them here.

I. _____

_____

II. _____

_____

Exercise 1 · Listening for Stressed Syllables

▶ Listen to the word your teacher says. Repeat the word.

▶ Count the syllables and write the number of syllables in the first column.

▶ Listen as your teacher says the word again. Identify the stressed syllable.

▶ Write the letters for the stressed syllable in the correct column.

	How many syllables do you hear?	First Syllable	Second Syllable
1.			
2.			
3.			
4.			
5.			

Unit 16 · Lesson 10

Exercise 2 · Sort It

▶ Read the skating terms in the **Word Bank**.

▶ Sort the words according to how they are used—**nouns**, **verbs**, or **adjectives**.

▶ Use the text selections **"Extreme Athletes"** and **"Tony Hawk: Extreme Athlete"** for context clues if you need help.

▶ **Hint:** Some words will fit in more than one category.

▶ The first one is done for you.

Word Bank

jump	safe	extreme	athlete	coping
athletic	trick	jump	competitive	medal
helmet	landing	crossover	ramps	compete

Nouns	Verbs	Adjectives
jump	jump	

Exercise 3 · Paraphrase It: Sentences for an Introductory Paragraph

▸ Paraphrase the last two main ideas on the **Blueprint for Writing: Outline**.

▸ Record them here.

III. _____

_____

IV. _____

_____

Exercise 4 · Write It: Introductory Paragraph for a Multiparagraph Composition

▸ Write your introductory paragraph.

▸ Read the multiparagraph composition with your teacher.

_____

_____

_____

_____

_____

(continued)

Tony Hawk began his skateboarding career as a child. A skateboard company sponsored him when he was 12. He turned pro when he was 14. He was ranked number one in the world at 16. By the time he was 33, he had won 73 out of 100 skateboarding competitions.

Hawk earned a lot of money in the initial years of his career. As a senior in high school, he bought his first house. His second home was purchased two years later. Hawk traveled around the world. He even paid for vacations for his buddies. He spent a lot of money keeping his electronic equipment updated.

Unfortunately, the monetary rewards didn't last. Skateboarding became less popular in the early nineties. Hawk's success declined. He had to sell one house and was forced to arrange for a cheaper payment on the other. He started a skateboarding company, but it did not prosper. Through these difficult times, Hawk questioned his future in skateboarding and considered alternative careers.

Hawk became successful again. Skateboarding became popular once more. His company began to prosper. Hawk signed sizable endorsements. He worked with an electronics company to produce a skateboarding video game. He even wrote a book about his life. In an effort to support skateboarders around the country, he gives money for the construction of skateboarding parks. While he has stopped competing, he still enjoys skating for fun.

Tony Hawk persisted through a career of highs and lows. Success came early in his career, but was followed by difficult times. He never gave up and his success grew again when skateboarding surged in popularity. Through many ups and downs, Hawk continued to strive for excellence on and off the skateboard. He has set a good example of persistence for many younger skaters.

Check off the activities you complete with each lesson. Evaluate your accomplishments at the end of each lesson. Pay attention to teacher evaluations and comments.

Unit Objectives	Lesson 1 (Date:_____)	Lesson 2 (Date:_____)
STEP 1 **Phonemic Awareness and Phonics** • Segment and delete syllables from multisyllable words. • Say vowel sounds: /ī/, /ĭ/, /ē/. • Identify **y** as a vowel. • Identify stressed syllables.	❑ Introduction: The Letter **y** ❑ Exercise 1: Listening for Sounds in Words	❑ Phoneme Segmentation ❑ Multiple Ways to Spell Vowel Sounds ❑ Listening for Sounds in Words
STEP 2 **Word Recognition and Spelling** • Spell two-syllable words with **y** as a vowel. • Read and spell the **Essential Words**: *answer, certain, engine, laugh, oil, poor.* • Read and spell words with prefixes **trans-** and **con-** and suffix **-ly**. • Use the **Change y Rule**.	❑ Exercise 2: Spelling Pretest 1 ❑ Memorize It	❑ Exercise 1: Sort It: Vowel Sounds for **y** ❑ Introduction: The **Change y Rule** ❑ Change It: The **Change y Rule** (T) ❑ Word Fluency 1 ❑ Memorize It ❑ Handwriting Practice
STEP 3 **Vocabulary and Morphology** • Identify antonyms, synonyms, word attributes, and analogies. • Identify comparative and superlative adjectives. • Use the meanings of prefixes to define words. • Add suffixes to words to change parts of speech.	❑ Unit Vocabulary ❑ K-W-L Organizer (T) ❑ Expression of the Day	❑ Exercise 2: Rewrite It: Comparative and Superlative Adjectives ❑ Expression of the Day
STEP 4 **Grammar and Usage** • Identify possessive forms. • Identify and use adverbs. • Identify **do** as a main or helping verb. • Analyze sentences with direct and indirect objects.	❑ Exercise 3: Rewrite It: Possessive Nouns ❑ Exercise 4: Identify It: Pronouns	❑ Exercise 3: Find It: Adverbs
STEP 5 **Listening and Reading Comprehension** • Use context-based strategies to define words. • Identify signal words for comprehension: **organize, outline, arrange**. • Identify main ideas and details.	❑ Exercise 5: Phrase It ❑ Independent Text: "The Pyramids"	❑ Passage Fluency 1 ❑ Exercise 4: Use the Clues
STEP 6 **Speaking and Writing** • Organize main ideas and details for writing. • Apply outline to writing introductory and body paragraphs.	❑ Masterpiece Sentences: Stages 1–3 ❑ Sentence Types: Fact or Opinion?	❑ Exercise 5: Rewrite It: Pronouns
Self-Evaluation (5 is the highest) **Effort** = I produced my best work. **Participation** = I was actively involved in tasks. **Independence** = I worked on my own.	**Effort:** 1 2 3 4 5 **Participation:** 1 2 3 4 5 **Independence:** 1 2 3 4 5	**Effort:** 1 2 3 4 5 **Participation:** 1 2 3 4 5 **Independence:** 1 2 3 4 5
Teacher Evaluation	**Effort:** 1 2 3 4 5 **Participation:** 1 2 3 4 5 **Independence:** 1 2 3 4 5	**Effort:** 1 2 3 4 5 **Participation:** 1 2 3 4 5 **Independence:** 1 2 3 4 5

Lesson 3 (Date:_____)	Lesson 4 (Date:_____)	Lesson 5 (Date:_____)
❑ Phoneme Segmentation ❑ Phoneme Substitution ❑ Syllable Awareness: Segmentation ❑ Exercise 1: Listening for Sounds in Words	❑ Exercise 1: Syllable Awareness: Segmentation	❑ Content Mastery: Syllable Awareness
❑ Exercise 2: Sort It: Syllable Types ❑ Exercise 3: Find It: Essential Words ❑ Word Fluency 1	❑ Change It: The **Change y Rule** (T) ❑ Word Fluency 2 ❑ Type It: Essential Words	❑ Content Mastery: Spelling Posttest 1
❑ Exercise 4: Define It ❑ Draw It: Idioms ❑ Expression of the Day	❑ Introduction: Adverb Suffix -ly ❑ Exercise 2: Find It: Adverbs ❑ Exercise 3: Rewrite It: Adverbs ❑ Expression of the Day	❑ Introduction: Analogies ❑ Exercise 1: Word Networks: Analogies ❑ Draw It: Idioms ❑ Expression of the Day
❑ Introduction: The Verb *Do* ❑ Exercise 5: Identify It: Main Verb or Helping Verb	❑ Exercise 4: Find It: Irregular Past Tense ❑ Tense Timeline (T) ❑ Exercise 5: Rewrite It: Verb Tense	❑ Masterpiece Sentences: Stage 2: Paint Your Predicate
❑ Instructional Text: "Building a Pyramid" (T) ❑ Exercise 6: Use the Clues	❑ Exercise 6: Blueprint for Reading: Main Ideas and Transition Words (T)	❑ Exercise 6: Blueprint for Reading: Identifying Details (T) (from Lesson 4)
❑ Exercise 7: Answer It	❑ Exercise 7: Blueprint for Writing: Outline (T) ❑ Exercise 8: Write It: Introductory Paragraph ❑ Challenge Text: "The Study of Mummies"	❑ Exercise 7: Blueprint for Writing: Outline (T) (from Lesson 4) ❑ Exercise 2: Write It: Multiparagraph Composition ❑ Challenge Text: "The Study of Mummies"
Effort: 1 2 3 4 5 **Participation:** 1 2 3 4 5 **Independence:** 1 2 3 4 5	**Effort:** 1 2 3 4 5 **Participation:** 1 2 3 4 5 **Independence:** 1 2 3 4 5	**Effort:** 1 2 3 4 5 **Participation:** 1 2 3 4 5 **Independence:** 1 2 3 4 5
Effort: 1 2 3 4 5 **Participation:** 1 2 3 4 5 **Independence:** 1 2 3 4 5	**Effort:** 1 2 3 4 5 **Participation:** 1 2 3 4 5 **Independence:** 1 2 3 4 5	**Effort:** 1 2 3 4 5 **Participation:** 1 2 3 4 5 **Independence:** 1 2 3 4 5

Check off the activities you complete with each lesson. Evaluate your accomplishments at the end of each lesson. Pay attention to teacher evaluations and comments.

	Unit Objectives	Lesson 6 (Date:_____)	Lesson 7 (Date:_____)
STEP 1	**Phonemic Awareness and Phonics** • Segment and delete syllables from multisyllable words. • Say vowel sounds: / ī /, / ĭ /, / ē /. • Identify **y** as a vowel. • Identify stressed syllables.	❏ Exercise 1: Listening for Stressed Syllables	❏ Exercise 1: Listening for Stressed Syllables ❏ Exercise 2: Listening for Word Parts
STEP 2	**Word Recognition and Spelling** • Spell two-syllable words with **y** as a vowel. • Read and spell the **Essential Words**: *answer, certain, engine, laugh, oil, poor*. • Read and spell words with prefixes **trans-** and **con-** and suffix **-ly**. • Use the **Change y Rule**.	❏ Exercise 2: Spelling Pretest 2 ❏ Word Fluency 3	❏ Word Fluency 4 ❏ Exercise 3: Build It: Prefixed Words
STEP 3	**Vocabulary and Morphology** • Identify antonyms, synonyms, word attributes, and analogies. • Identify comparative and superlative adjectives. • Use the meanings of prefixes to define words. • Add suffixes to words to change parts of speech.	❏ Unit Vocabulary ❏ K-W-L Organizer (T) ❏ Expression of the Day	❏ Introduction: Prefixes **con-** and **trans-** ❏ Exercise 4: Define It: Prefixes **con-** and **trans-** ❏ Expression of the Day
STEP 4	**Grammar and Usage** • Identify possessive forms. • Identify and use adverbs. • Identify **do** as a main or helping verb. • Analyze sentences with direct and indirect objects.	❏ Introduction: Indirect Objects ❏ Exercise 3: Identify It: Direct and Indirect Objects ❏ Exercise 4: Find It: Direct and Indirect Objects	❏ Exercise 5: Find It: Indirect Objects ❏ Exercise 6: Rewrite It: Indirect Objects
STEP 5	**Listening and Reading Comprehension** • Use context-based strategies to define words. • Identify signal words for comprehension: **organize, outline, arrange**. • Identify main ideas and details.	❏ Exercise 5: Phrase It ❏ Independent Text: "Living in Egypt" ❏ Exercise 6: Use the Clues	❏ Passage Fluency 2
STEP 6	**Speaking and Writing** • Organize main ideas and details for writing. • Apply outline to writing introductory and body paragraphs.	❏ Exercise 7: Rewrite It: Pronouns	❏ Exercise 7: Rewrite It
	Self-Evaluation (5 is the highest) **Effort** = I produced my best work. **Participation** = I was actively involved in tasks. **Independence** = I worked on my own.	**Effort:** 1 2 3 4 5 **Participation:** 1 2 3 4 5 **Independence:** 1 2 3 4 5	**Effort:** 1 2 3 4 5 **Participation:** 1 2 3 4 5 **Independence:** 1 2 3 4 5
	Teacher Evaluation	**Effort:** 1 2 3 4 5 **Participation:** 1 2 3 4 5 **Independence:** 1 2 3 4 5	**Effort:** 1 2 3 4 5 **Participation:** 1 2 3 4 5 **Independence:** 1 2 3 4 5

Lesson 8 (Date:_____)	Lesson 9 (Date:_____)	Lesson 10 (Date:_____)
❏ Exercise 1: Listening for Word Parts	❏ Exercise 1: Listening for Stressed Syllables	❏ Exercise 1: Listening for Stressed Syllables
❏ Exercise 2: Divide It	❏ Exercise 2: Build It	❏ Content Mastery: Spelling Posttest 2
❏ Content Mastery: Word Relationships ❏ Content Mastery: Suffixes	❏ Introduction: Forms of the Prefix **con-** ❏ Exercise 3: Define It: Forms of the Prefix **con-** ❏ Exercise 4: Fill-In: Forms of the Prefix **con-**	❏ Exercise 2: Sort It: Meaning Categories ❏ Expression of the Day
❏ Exercise 3: Diagram It: Indirect Objects	❏ Exercise 5: Find It: Indirect Objects	❏ Content Mastery: Possessive Nouns; Adverbs; *Do*—Main Verb or Helpling Verb; Indirect Objects
❏ Instructional Text: "Growing Up Egyptian" ❏ Exercise 4: Use the Clues	❏ Exercise 6: Blueprint for Reading: Main Ideas (T)	❏ Exercise 6: Blueprint for Reading: Identifying Details (T) (Lesson 9)
❏ Exercise 5: Answer It	❏ Exercise 7: Blueprint for Writing: Outline (T) ❏ Exercise 8: Write It: Introductory Paragraph ❏ Challenge Text: "King Tut: Egyptian Pharaoh"	❏ Exercise 7: Blueprint for Writing: Outline (T) (Lesson 9) ❏ Exercise 3: Write It: Multiparagraph Composition (T) ❏ Challenge Text: "King Tut: Egyptian Pharaoh"
Effort: 1 2 3 4 5 **Participation:** 1 2 3 4 5 **Independence:** 1 2 3 4 5	**Effort:** 1 2 3 4 5 **Participation:** 1 2 3 4 5 **Independence:** 1 2 3 4 5	**Effort:** 1 2 3 4 5 **Participation:** 1 2 3 4 5 **Independence:** 1 2 3 4 5
Effort: 1 2 3 4 5 **Participation:** 1 2 3 4 5 **Independence:** 1 2 3 4 5	**Effort:** 1 2 3 4 5 **Participation:** 1 2 3 4 5 **Independence:** 1 2 3 4 5	**Effort:** 1 2 3 4 5 **Participation:** 1 2 3 4 5 **Independence:** 1 2 3 4 5

Exercise 1 · Listening for Sounds in Words

▸ Listen to each word your teacher says.

▸ Put an X in the column to show what vowel sound you hear.

	Long i	Long e	Short i
1.			
2.			
3.			
4.			
5.			
6.			
7.			
8.			
9.			
10.			

Exercise 2 · Spelling Pretest 1

▸ Write the word your teacher repeats.

1. _____
2. _____
3. _____
4. _____
5. _____

6. _____
7. _____
8. _____
9. _____
10. _____

11. _____
12. _____
13. _____
14. _____
15. _____

Exercise 3 · Rewrite It: Possessive Nouns

▸ Read each sentence.

▸ Change the underlined words in each sentence to show the possessive form.

▸ Write the possessive form of each phrase on the line.

1. The base of the pyramid had four corners. _____

2. Workers chipped and carved the shape of each stone. _____

3. The waters of the Nile were used to move the stone. _____

4. The tools of the workers were chisels and stone hammers. _____

5. Pyramids were used for the graves of kings. _____

6. The weight of one block was fifteen tons. _____

7. The methods of the workers involved many steps. _____

8. The day of the worker was long and hard. _____

9. Today we can see the glory of the pyramids. _____

10. We marvel at the construction of the pyramid. _____

Unit 17 · Lesson 1

Exercise 4 · Identify It: Pronouns

▸ Read each sentence.

▸ Decide if the underlined pronoun is a nominative, object, or possessive pronoun.

▸ Copy the pronoun into the correct column below.

1. People of Egypt are proud the pyramids are <u>theirs</u>.

2. <u>They</u> offer trips by camel to see them.

3. That book with photos of Egypt is <u>mine</u>.

4. The men showed the blocks the stonecutters made to <u>us</u>.

5. Their way of building is different from <u>ours</u>.

6. A stonecutter sharpened the tools that were <u>his</u>.

7. He kept <u>them</u> in a safe place.

8. <u>He</u> would give his son his tools.

9. A father would offer his son help to use <u>them</u>.

10. <u>You</u> should visit the pyramids too.

(continued)

Exercise 4 (continued) · **Identify It: Pronouns**

	Nominative	Object	Possessive
1.			
2.			
3.			
4.			
5.			
6.			
7.			
8.			
9.			
10.			

Unit 17 · Lesson 1

Exercise 5 · Phrase It

▸ Use the penciling strategy to "scoop" the phrases in each sentence.

▸ Read the sentences as you would speak them.

▸ The first two are done for you as examples.

1. The pyramids were constructed long ago.

2. It seems like an impossible task.

3. They made huge numbers of blocks.

4. One base block was big.

5. Their method involved steps.

6. First, they dug the stone.

7. Then, it was put on a raft.

8. The raft drifted down the Nile River.

9. At the site, the stone was taken off.

10. Workers carved a channel into the stone.

Exercise 1 · Sort It: Vowel Sounds for y

▶ Read the words in the **Word Bank**.

▶ Sort the words according to the vowel sound represented by the letter **y**.

▶ Write the word under the correct heading.

Word Bank

type	army	copy	byte
dry	happy	party	hype
rye	by	story	tiny

long i	long e

Unit 17 · Lesson 2

Exercise 2 · Rewrite It: Comparative and Superlative Adjectives

▶ Read the adjectives.

▶ Add **-er** or **more** to make the comparative form of the adjective.

▶ Add **-est** or **most** to make the superlative form of the adjective.

▶ Use the **Change y Rule** when necessary.

	Adjective	Comparative	Superlative
1.	dark	_____	_____
2.	western	_____	_____
3.	carsick	_____	_____
4.	silly	_____	_____
5.	happy	_____	_____

What job does the word with the **-er** suffix have?

_____

What job does the word with the **-est** suffix have?

_____

When do we use **more** and **most** with the adjective?

_____

_____

Write two sentences using comparative and superlative adjectives from the task above.

_____

_____

_____

_____

Exercise 3 · Find It: Adverbs

▸ Read each sentence.

▸ Find and underline the adverb or prepositional phrase that acts like an adverb in each sentence.

▸ Decide if the word or phrase tells **how**, **when**, or **where**.

▸ Mark the correct column to show your choice.

	how	when	where
1. The Egyptian pyramids were built in the desert.			
2. Huge stone blocks were piled on top of each other.			
3. The workers hammered the stones forcefully.			
4. All year long, the work continued.			
5. Expert workers shaped the stones precisely.			
6. The stone cracked unexpectedly.			
7. Workers sculpted the stones into shapes.			
8. The huge stones fell through the base.			
9. The stone split with a loud crack.			
10. Stone fragments gashed workers on their arms.			

Unit 17 · Lesson 2

Exercise 4 · Use the Clues

▸ Read the sentence pairs.

▸ Read the pronoun that is circled.

▸ Identify the noun that the pronoun replaces in each sentence.

▸ Underline the noun replaced by the pronoun.

▸ Draw an arrow to show the link between the pronoun and the noun it replaces.

1. (It) was made long ago. It's a pyramid!

2. Why were pyramids constructed? First, (they) were sacred sites.

3. They drenched the wedge in water. (It) expanded.

4. At last, the stone split. They cut (it).

5. (It) was finished. One more amazing pyramid!

Exercise 5 · Rewrite It: Pronouns

▸ Reread each pair of sentences in Exercise 4, **Use the Clues**.

▸ Replace the circled pronoun with the noun or noun phrase that it represents.

▸ Rewrite the sentence using the noun.

▸ Check for sentence signals—capital letters, commas, and end punctuation.

▸ Read the new sentence.

1. _____

2. _____

3. _____

4. _____

5. _____

Exercise 1 · Listening for Sounds in Words

▶ Listen to each word your teacher says.

▶ Put an X in the column to indicate which long vowel sound you hear.

	/ ē /	/ ī /
1.		
2.		
3.		
4.		
5.		
6.		
7.		
8.		
9.		
10.		

Exercise 2 · Sort It: Syllable Types

▸ Read the syllables in the **Word Bank**.

▸ Sort the syllables according to their syllable type.

▸ Write each syllable under the correct heading.

Word Bank

cop	byte	my	y	gym
ar	prop	type	ti	tem
er	rye	ny	ty	sys

closed	final silent <u>e</u>	open	<u>r</u>-controlled

Unit 17 · Lesson 3

Exercise 3 · Find It: Essential Words

▸ Find the **Essential Words** for this unit in these sentences.

▸ Underline them. There may be more than one in a sentence.

▸ Use your **Essential Word Cards** if you need help.

1. Type your answer quickly.

2. Make certain that fence is on your property.

3. Why is the oil all over the engine?

4. I had to laugh when the mummy came to the door.

5. The poor baby needed to be held.

▸ Write the **Essential Words** in the spaces.

_____   _____   _____

_____   _____   _____

Exercise 4 · Define It

▶ Fill in the blanks with a category and an attribute to define the word.

▶ Compare definitions that you're unsure of with a dictionary definition.

▶ Do the first word with your teacher.

1. A **pyramid** is _____ that _____
                              category   attribute(s)

   _____.

2. An **army** is _____ who _____
                             category   attribute(s)

   _____.

3. An **eye** is _____ that _____

   _____.

4. **Happy** is _____ that _____

   _____.

5. A **lady** is _____ who _____

   _____.

6. A **party** is _____ that _____

   _____.

7. An **engine** is _____ that _____

   _____.

8. A **bunny** is _____ that _____

   _____.

9. A **contract** is _____ that _____

   _____.

10. A **pony** is _____ that _____

   _____.

(continued)

Unit 17 • Lesson 3

Exercise 4 (continued) • Define It

Write the vocabulary words that are examples of **mammals**.

▸ Write the words in the blanks.

_____   _____   _____

_____   _____

Exercise 5 • Identify It: Main Verb or Helping Verb

▸ Read each sentence.

▸ Underline the verb or verb phrase in each sentence.

▸ Decide if the verb **do** is used as a main verb or a helping verb.

▸ Fill in the correct bubble to show your choice.

▸ Do the first sentence with your teacher.

	Main Verb	Helping Verb
1. The Egyptians did build the pyramids.	◯	◯
2. In those days, men did all the work by hand.	◯	◯
3. The pyramids do have four sides.	◯	◯
4. Some do their work quickly.	◯	◯
5. All the men do their jobs with commitment.	◯	◯
6. A raft does transport cargo on the Nile.	◯	◯
7. The workers did complete repairs on the sites.	◯	◯
8. One stonecutter does his trade extremely well.	◯	◯
9. They will be doing more repairs in the future.	◯	◯
10. The students did study for their test about the pyramids.	◯	◯

Exercise 6 · Use the Clues

▶ Use context clues to define **trenches**.

▶ Underline the vocabulary word.

▶ Read text surrounding the unknown word.

▶ Put a box around the synonym for **trenches**.

---

from "Building a Pyramid"

Next, the ground and building materials were prepared. The ground had to be leveled before any stones were placed. To do this, the Egyptians cut a series of trenches into the land. They flooded these ditches with water. Water acted like a level. The workers cut the earth "islands" between the trenches to match the level of the water. Next, the Egyptians cut giant stone blocks.

▶ Write a definition based on the context clues.

▶ Verify your definition with the dictionary or www.yourdictionary.com.

Trenches: _____

Exercise 7 · Answer It

▸ Underline the signal word in the question.

▸ Write the answer in complete sentences.

1. Organize the items in the following list into the order they appear in the text. Pyramids were built:

   a. near a waterway

   b. in the west

   c. close to a quarry

   1. _____

   2. _____

   3. _____

2. Before building a pyramid, workers used a series of steps to level the ground before any stones were placed. Use the text to arrange the following steps into the correct sequence.

   a. dug the earth between the trenches to match the level of water

   b. flooded ditches with water

   c. dug a series of trenches

   1. _____

   2. _____

   3. _____

(continued)

Exercise 7 (continued) · Answer It

3. Throughout the article, the author cites several intriguing facts involving the Egyptian pyramids. Select three intriguing facts about the pyramids. Explain why these facts are intriguing to you.

_____

_____

_____

_____

_____

_____

_____

4. Egyptians considered the shape of the pyramid to be a symbol. Describe the meanings of this symbol mentioned in this article.

_____

_____

_____

Exercise 1 · Syllable Awareness: Segmentation

▸ Listen to the word your teacher says.

▸ Count the syllables. Write the number in the first column.

▸ Write the letter and diacritical mark to stand for each vowel sound you hear.

- Mark short vowel sounds with a breve (˘).

- Mark long vowel sounds with a macron (¯).

- For **r**-controlled vowel sounds, mark the vowel before the **r** with a circumflex (ˆ).

	How many syllables do you hear?	First vowel sound	Second vowel sound	Third vowel sound	Fourth vowel sound
1.					
2.					
3.					
4.					
5.					
6.					
7.					
8.					
9.					
10.					

Exercise 2 · Find It: Adverbs

▸ Each sentence contains an adverb ending in **-ly**.

▸ Underline the adverb and draw an arrow from the adverb to the verb it modifies.
Hint: Adverbs do not have to be next to the verb they modify.

Sentences	Answer the question.
Example: Luis <u>quickly</u> answered the ringing phone.	How did Luis answer? **quickly**
Example: His friend Hakim asked him <u>politely</u> if he wanted to watch a video with his family.	How did Hakim ask? **politely**
Example: Now his father had <u>gladly</u> rented another old film.	How did his father rent? **gladly**
1. The boys had recently studied about mummies from ancient Egypt in school.	When did the boys study?
2. Happily, they found an old horror movie called *The Mummy*.	How did they find the movie?
3. The action of the film began calmly enough in Egypt in 1921.	In what way did the action begin?
4. After digging for several months, an archeologist, Sir Joseph Wemple, finally discovered a mummy in a crypt.	When did Wemple discover the mummy?
5. The ancient Egyptians preserved this mummy's body perfectly.	How did they preserve the body?

Unit 17 · Lesson 4

Exercise 3 · Rewrite It: Adverbs

▸ Underline the prepositional phrase that begins with **in** and ends in **way**.

▸ Change the adjective that modifies **way** into an adverb by adding **-ly**.

▸ Say the sentence with an adverb instead of the underlined prepositional phrase.

▸ Write the adverb made from the adjective in the column titled **Adverb**.

Sentence	Adverb
Example: In a quick way, I went back to my homework to read about cats in ancient Egypt.	quickly
1. Ancient Egyptians treated cats in a wonderful way.	
2. They wanted to respect cats for the job they did killing the mice in a rapid way, which protected the stored grain.	
3. In a real way, all cats were property of the Pharaoh.	
4. It was a crime to harm a cat even in a mistaken way.	
5. A person who harmed a cat was punished in a bad way.	

Exercise 4 · Find It: Irregular Past Tense

▸ Read the text below, adapted from **"Building a Pyramid."**

▸ Find and underline all the irregular past tense verbs.

▸ Copy the irregular past tense verbs on the lines below.

---

based on "Building a Pyramid"

The pyramids were constructed long ago. They took a long time to build. Men worked hard and time flew. The workers did not have wheels or many tools. Sometimes they lent each other their tools. If a worker mistook directions, he placed stones incorrectly. When the pyramids were complete, they stood in the desert and shone in the sun for all to see. The pyramids have withstood the passing of time well.

_____   _____   _____

_____   _____   _____

_____   _____   _____

_____

Exercise 5 · Rewrite It: Verb Tense

▸ Read the five sentences.

▸ Write the verb under the correct position on the **Tense Timeline**.

▸ Expand the verb to include the two additional verb forms on the **Tense Timeline**, following your teacher's example.

Past	Present	Future
Yesterday	Today	Tomorrow

1. Stonecutters **do** their tasks with great skill.

2. Workers **lent** their tools to each other.

3. He **will do** the extra work.

4. Birds **flew** over the pyramids.

5. The worker **will lend** his hammer.

Exercise 6 · Blueprint for Reading: Main Ideas and Transition Words

▸ Highlight the main ideas in blue.

▸ Circle the transition words.

---

based on "Building a Pyramid"

Egypt's pyramids are true engineering feats. No written records survive to explain how the pyramids were built. Archaeologists have found valuable clues about the Egyptians' methods.

To start, Egyptians identified the pyramid's site. Ancient Egyptians built their tombs in the western part of the country. In addition, a pyramid had to be close to a quarry. This would be the source for the stone. The quarry had to be near the construction zone. In those days, there were no trucks or trains to transport the heavy stones. All of the stones were moved by people. Finally, the pyramid had to be near a waterway. Boats brought in the other types of rock used in the pyramid. Limestone, granite, and alabaster were all imported. A docking harbor has been uncovered near the Great Pyramid.

Next, the ground and building materials were prepared. The ground had to be leveled before any stones were placed. Next, the Egyptians cut giant stone blocks. These blocks would be used to build the pyramid. The builders drew sections onto a stone surface. To remove the stone, they drove wooden

(continued)

wedges into the rock. They soaked these wedges with water. The wedges expanded. They split the rock. The workers cut the blocks into the desired shape. They used copper chisels and stone hammers to make the cuts.

As construction began, the ancient Egyptians worked hard to achieve precision. They did this by using only simple tools. The builders had to be sure the stones for the base of the pyramid were placed in a straight line. They drilled holes in the stones at regular intervals. These went all around the base. They put a stake into each hole. The stakes made reference lines. Traces of these markings remain. Builders used these reference lines for another purpose. The builders marked midpoints on the base. These marks would help in the placement of stones.

As the pyramid rose, the Egyptians had to create ways to lift the huge stones into place. Each stone had to be moved from the quarry to the construction site. Once the block arrived at the pyramid, it had to be lifted into place. To do this, the Egyptians used ramps. A huge ramp extended from the quarry. This ramp wrapped around the pyramid as it rose. Eventually, it encased the entire pyramid. It was made of rubble (limestone chips) and *tafla* (chalky clay). The ramp was designed so that the huge stone blocks did not press against the pyramid. To position the enormous blocks, many workers dragged them up the ramps. They did not yet have a wheel. The workers probably pushed the blocks on special platforms called sledges.

Exercise 7 · Blueprint for Writing: Outline

_____

I. _____

   A. _____

   B. _____

   C. _____

   D. _____

II. _____

   A. _____

   B. _____

   C. _____

   D. _____

III. _____

   A. _____

   B. _____

   C. _____

   D. _____

IV. _____

   A. _____

   B. _____

   C. _____

   D. _____

_____

Exercise 8 · Write It: Introductory Paragraph

▸ Read the topic sentence.

▸ Paraphrase the main ideas from the **Blueprint for Writing: Outline** to add to the introductory paragraph frame.

▸ Read the entire paragraph.

The ancient Egyptians used a series of creative methods to build the pyramids. First,

_____.

Then, _____.

Next, _____.

Finally, _____.

These methods were amazing, given the ancient times when the pyramids were built.

Exercise 1 · Word Networks: Analogies

▸ Read the first word pair.

▸ Underline the relationship between these two words: **synonym**, **antonym**, **attribute**.

▸ Choose a word from the **Word Bank** to complete the analogy with a similar relationship.

▸ Write the word.

▸ Discuss the analogies with a partner.

Word Bank

rely	pretty	colt	tiny	byte
contrast	big	system	pony	harmony

Analogy	Relationship		
1. happy: sad :: ugly: _____	synonym	antonym	attribute
2. transmit: send :: plan: _____	synonym	antonym	attribute
3. poor: rich :: conflict: _____	synonym	antonym	attribute
4. measure: inch :: memory _____	synonym	antonym	attribute
5. adult: horse :: baby: _____	synonym	antonym	attribute
6. hop: rabbit :: gallop: _____	synonym	antonym	attribute
7. byte: small :: gigabyte: _____	synonym	antonym	attribute
8. huge: big :: small: _____	synonym	antonym	attribute
9. answer: question :: compare: _____	synonym	antonym	attribute
10. imply: infer :: depend: _____	synonym	antonym	attribute

Exercise 2 · Write It: Multiparagraph Composition

▸ Rewrite your introductory paragraph from Lesson 4, Exercise 8.

▸ Use your **Blueprint for Writing: Outline** to write the first body paragraph with your teacher.

▸ Finish writing the composition on your own.

▸ Read the entire composition, including the conclusion provided on the next page.

Introduction
_____
_____
_____
_____
_____
_____

(continued)

Exercise 2 (continued) · Write It: Multiparagraph Composition

Body 1

_____

_____

_____

_____

Body 2

_____

_____

_____

_____

Body 3

_____

_____

_____

_____

Body 4

_____

_____

_____

_____

Conclusion

The pyramids were marvels of human engineering. Many pyramids still stand as examples of ancient Egyptian ingenuity and hard work.

Exercise 1 · Listening for Stressed Syllables

▸ Listen to the word your teacher says.

▸ Repeat the word.

▸ Listen for the stressed, or accented, syllable.

▸ Mark an X in the box to mark the position of the stressed, or accented, syllable.

Word	First Syllable	Second Syllable	Third Syllable	Fourth Syllable
1. deny				
2. copy				
3. density				
4. priority				
5. exactly				

Exercise 2 · Spelling Pretest 2

▸ Write the word your teacher repeats.

1. _____   6. _____   11. _____

2. _____   7. _____   12. _____

3. _____   8. _____   13. _____

4. _____   9. _____   14. _____

5. _____   10. _____   15. _____

Exercise 3 · Identify It: Direct and Indirect Objects

▸ Reread each sentence.

▸ Decide if the underlined noun is a direct object or an indirect object.

▸ Put an X in the correct column.

	Indirect Object	Direct Object
1. Helpers bring the <u>workers</u> their lunch.		
2. The father handed Hebeny the scribe's <u>pen</u>.		
3. The boss forgave <u>Moses</u> his mistake.		
4. The king granted the men <u>freedom</u>.		
5. The elders tell young Egyptian <u>boys</u> stories.		

Exercise 4 · Find It: Direct and Indirect Objects

▸ Read each sentence.

▸ Find and underline the indirect object and direct object.

▸ Copy the indirect object and direct object into the correct column.

	Indirect Object	Direct Object
1. The bosses gave the men a master plan.		
2. The rafts brought the stonecutters large blocks.		
3. The stonecutter lent the worker his tools.		
4. Almost always, a scribe handed his son his job.		
5. Their jobs gave scribes many unusual favors.		

Unit 17 · Lesson 6

Exercise 5 · Phrase It

▸ Use the penciling strategy to "scoop" the phrases in each sentence.

▸ Read the sentence as you would speak it.

▸ The first two are done for you.

1. In Egypt, the public depends on farmers.

2. They supply all the crops.

3. The Nile River floods from June to September.

4. Their lands are covered with water.

5. When the river floods, they still have to work.

6. Many farmers work on pyramids.

7. Hebeny's father is a scribe.

8. It is one job that requires a formal education.

9. The writing is done with a code.

10. Hebeny wants to be like her dad.

Exercise 6 · Use the Clues

‣ Read the sentence pairs.

‣ Read the pronoun that is circled.

‣ Identify the noun that the pronoun replaces in each sentence.

‣ Underline the noun replaced by the pronoun.

‣ Draw an arrow to show the link between the pronoun and the noun it replaces.

1. First, meet Moses. (He's) a farmer's son.

2. In Egypt, the public depends on farmers. (They) supply all the crops.

3. Moses helps his dad. He gathers crops. He covers (them) to protect them.

4. Moses helps his dad. He gathers crops. (He) covers them to protect them.

5. Hebeny studies hard. (Her) father is a scribe.

Exercise 7 • Rewrite It: Pronouns

▸ Reread each pair of sentences in Exercise 6, **Use the Clues**.

▸ Replace the pronoun with the noun or noun phrase that it represents.

▸ Rewrite the sentence using the noun.

▸ Check for sentence signals—capital letters and end punctuation.

▸ Read the new sentence.

▸ Do the first one with your teacher.

1. _____

2. _____

3. _____

4. _____

5. _____

Exercise 1 · Listening for Stressed Syllables

▶ Listen to the word your teacher says. Repeat the word.

▶ Listen for the stressed, or accented, syllable.

▶ Put an X in the box to mark the position of the stressed, or accented, syllable.

Word	First Syllable	Second Syllable	Third Syllable	Fourth Syllable
1. fryer				
2. happy				
3. nobility				
4. enzyme				
5. synopsis				

Unit 17 · Lesson 7

Exercise 2 · Listening for Word Parts

▶ Listen to each word your teacher says.

▶ Mark **Yes** or **No** to show whether the word has a suffix.

▶ If **Yes**, write the suffix.

	Do you hear a suffix on the word?		If **Yes**, what is the suffix?
	Yes	No	
1.			
2.			
3.			
4.			
5.			
6.			
7.			
8.			
9.			
10.			

Exercise 3 · Build It: Prefixed Words

▸ Read the prefixes and syllables in the box.

▸ Combine the syllables with **con-** and **trans-** to make new words.

▸ Record the words on the lines.

▸ Check a dictionary to verify that words are real words.

con-	fuse	plant	form
trans-	mit	figure	gress

_____   _____   _____

_____   _____   _____

_____   _____   _____

Unit 17 · Lesson 7

Exercise 4 · Define It: Prefixes con- and trans-

▶ Record the meaning of the prefix **con-**.

▶ Use the definition of the prefix to help define the underlined word in each sentence.

▶ Fill in the blanks.

▶ Verify your definition with a dictionary.

1. **Con-** is a prefix meaning _____.

2. The word part **nect** means *join*. When you **connect** something you

   _____ something else.

3. The word part **fuse** can mean *melt* or *mix up*. **Confuse** means

   _____.

4. The word part **fine** can mean *to border*. **Confine** means _____.

5. The word **text** means *words*. **Context** means _____.

▶ Record the meaning of the prefix **trans-**.

▶ Use the definition of the prefix to help define the underlined word in each sentence.

▶ Fill in the blanks.

▶ Verify your definition with a dictionary.

6. **Trans-** is a prefix meaning _____.

7. A **transatlantic** flight flies _____.

8. The word part **port** means *carry*. When you **transport** goods across the ocean,

   you _____ across the ocean.

9. The word part **late** can also mean *to carry* or *bring*. When you **translate** a word

   from one language to another you _____

   _____.

10. The word part **fuse** can mean *to pour* or *to move a liquid*. When a doctor

    transfuses blood she moves it _____.

Exercise 5 · Find It: Indirect Objects

▸ Read each sentence.

▸ Find and underline the indirect object.

1. The scribe's job gave him respect in the community.

2. The worker handed him his tools.

3. Ancient Egyptians rarely gave them the chance to attend school.

4. The girl's mother sold her a fine robe.

5. The stonecutter showed us his work.

Exercise 6 · Rewrite It: Indirect Objects

▸ Read each sentence.

▸ Find and underline the indirect object.

▸ Replace the noun (indirect object) with a pronoun.

▸ Rewrite the sentence.

1. The scribe gave his son lessons.

   _____

2. Old tales tell modern people the history of long ago.

   _____

3. The teacher gave Maria and me a book and pencil for our report.

   _____

4. Our report must tell the class the story of the pyramids.

   _____

5. The teacher gave the report a good grade.

   _____

Exercise 7 · Rewrite It

▸ Read sentences from **"Living in Egypt."**

▸ Replace an underlined pronoun with a noun or an underlined noun with a pronoun.

▸ Rewrite the sentences.

▸ Read your sentences to the class.

1. At harvest time, <u>Moses</u> helps his dad.

_____

2. When the river floods, <u>they</u> still have to work.

_____

3. When the river gets back to normal, so do <u>they</u>.

_____

4. <u>Hebeny</u> studies hard.

_____

5. <u>She</u> wants to become a scribe.

_____

Exercise 1 · Listening for Word Parts

▸ Listen to each word your teacher says.

▸ Mark **Yes** or **No** to tell if you hear a suffix.

▸ If **Yes**, write the suffix.

	Do you hear a suffix on the word?		If **Yes**, what is the suffix?
	Yes	No	
1.			
2.			
3.			
4.			
5.			
6.			
7.			
8.			
9.			
10.			

Exercise 2 · Divide It

▸ Use the steps of **Divide It** to break the words into syllables.

▸ Blend the syllables together to read the word.

1. sloppy

2. ugly

3. levy

4. copy

5. navy

6. lazy

7. forty

8. army

9. ivy

10. imply

Unit 17 · Lesson 8

Exercise 3 · Diagram It: Indirect Objects

▸ Read each sentence.

▸ Diagram the first sentence with your teacher.

▸ Diagram the remaining sentences independently.

▸ Write an X above the vertical line that separates the complete subject from the complete predicate.

    1. The boy's father gave him lessons.

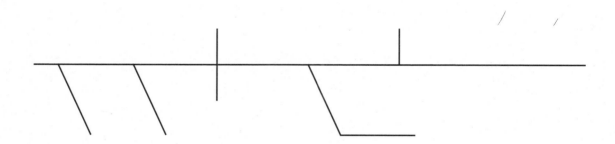

    2. Ancient Egyptians did not give girls many chances for education.

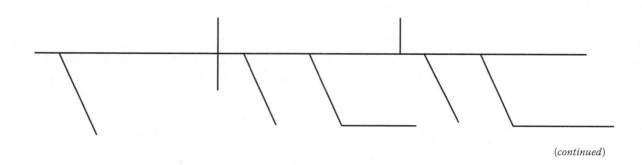

(continued)

Exercise 3 (continued) · Diagram It: Indirect Objects

3. The worker handed him his tools.

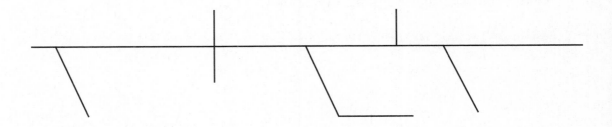

4. The girl's mother sold her a fine robe.

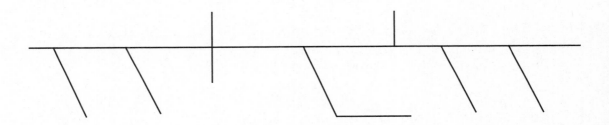

5. The stonecutter showed us his work.

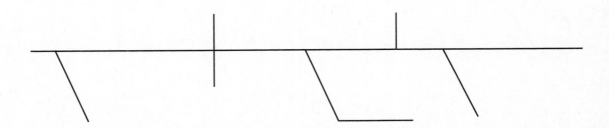

Exercise 4 · Use the Clues

▸ Use meaning signals to define **scribe**.

▸ Put a box around the vocabulary word.

▸ Look for the meaning signal: **parentheses ( )**.

▸ Read the text inside the parentheses ( ).

▸ Underline the words that help define the unknown word.

---

from "Growing Up Egyptian"

If you were a child in ancient Egypt, the size of your home depended on your father's job. Was he the pharaoh? Then your mud-brick home would be a palace with many rooms. Was he a nobleman or a scribe (one of the few people who could write)? If so, your large house may have had a private courtyard with flowers and a fish pond.

▸ Write a definition based on the context clues.

▸ Verify your definition with the dictionary or www.yourdictionary.com.

Scribe: _____

Exercise 5 · Answer It

▸ Underline the signal word in the question.

▸ Write the answers in complete sentences.

1. At the beginning of the article, the author provides four clues that describe growing up in ancient Egypt. List four clues that describe growing up in modern America.

   _____

   _____

2. Select the type of house that you would like to own if you lived in ancient Egypt. Tell what you would have to do in order to own that type of house. **Hint**: Be sure to consider your gender when answering.

   _____

   _____

   _____

   _____

   _____

(continued)

Exercise 5 (continued) · **Answer It**

3. Tell why it was difficult to learn the ancient Egyptian language.

_____

_____

_____

_____

4. Students practiced writing the hieroglyphic signs on a variety of surfaces. Outline the variety of surfaces used for writing.

I. _____

a) _____

b) _____

c) _____

5. Distinguish between your ability to make career choices and the ability of ancient Egyptian children to make career choices.

_____

_____

_____

_____

Exercise 1 · Listening for Stressed Syllables

▸ Listen to each word your teacher says. Repeat the word.

▸ Listen for the stressed, or accented, syllable.

▸ Put an X in the box to mark the position of the stressed, or accented, syllable.

Word	First Syllable	Second Syllable	Third Syllable
1. hypnosis			
2. sixty			
3. reply			
4. transact			
5. hurry			

Exercise 2 · Build It

▸ Combine the prefixes in the middle square with the base words.
  Example: com- + mit = commit

▸ Record the words in the chart that follows according to the prefix.

▸ Use a dictionary to verify that you are building real words.

form	verse	late
fer	com- con- col- trans-	mit
pose	gress	spire

(continued)

Exercise 2 (continued) · Build It

col-	com-	con-	trans-

Exercise 3 · Define It: Forms of the Prefix con-

▸ Fill in the blanks to complete the definitions of words using forms of **con-**.

▸ Use a dictionary for extra help if necessary.

1. The prefixes **con-**, **col-**, **cor-**, **co-**, and **com-** all mean

_____ or _____.

2. **Conjoined** twins are _____ each other or together.

3. When you **cosign** a contract, you _____ someone else.

4. The word part **lide** means *hit* or *strike*.

When two ships **collide**, they _____ each other.

5. The word part **rode** can mean *gnaw* or *chew* in the sense of being made into smaller pieces (not as something eaten). The prefix **cor-** can make a word more intense. When metal **corrodes** it becomes

_____.

Unit 17 · Lesson 9

Exercise 4 · Fill-In: Forms of the Prefix con-

▸ Use the prefix **con-** or one of its forms in the **Prefix Box** to complete the word in each sentence.

▸ Read the sentence to help you form the correct word.

▸ Use a dictionary to check the word.

▸ Copy the completed whole word.

Prefix Box

co-	col-	com-	con-	cor-

Sentence — Add the prefix	Write the word
Example: He won twenty dollars at the pie-eating __con__test.	contest
Example: My uncle's bakery was the __co__sponsor of the contest.	cosponsor
Example: You have to watch your __con__duct when you are in the public eye.	conduct
1. Luis studied the _____lapse of the Roman Empire last term.	
2. We had to _____pare and contrast the book to the movie.	
3. I finally _____pleted the report late last night.	
4. The salt water finally _____roded the body of Andy's car.	
5. Their _____stant partying drove their roommate crazy.	

Exercise 5 · Find It: Indirect Objects

▶ Listen and follow along as your teacher reads the text.

▶ Reread the text.

▶ Find and underline each indirect object.

▶ Circle each direct object.

based on "Building a Pyramid"

The rafts drifted slowly down the Nile. They brought the stonecutters the large blocks to cut. These blocks gave workers the material they needed to construct the pyramids. Slowly and carefully, blocks were cut and placed on top of each other according to a plan. Sometimes mistakes were made. The bosses did not forgive stonecutters their errors. Mistakes would cost men their jobs.

Today, history gives us facts about how the pyramids were made.

Exercise 6 · Blueprint for Reading: Main Ideas

▶ Highlight the main ideas in blue.

based on "Growing Up Egyptian"

Education

In ancient Egypt, only a few children went to school. If you were lucky enough to go to school, you studied to become a scribe. Scribes were very important people in ancient Egypt because they were almost the only ones who could read and write. Although records tell us there were a few female scribes, most were men. Boys entered scribal school when they were quite young, and they had to study hard for about 10 to 12 years.

Learning the ancient Egyptian language was difficult. Ancient Egyptians did not use an alphabet; instead, they used hundreds of picture symbols to represent words. These symbols, called *hieroglyphs*, were complicated. Young scribes spent years learning the hieroglyph writing system. Scribes also had to learn how to write *hieratic*. This was a shorthand script they used for everyday writing.

(continued)

Students learned about more than just language in scribal school. They practiced writing by copying things that had already been written: letters, literature, and religious records. They copied business and government documents. As they copied, they learned about the subjects of all these documents. Students practiced the hieroglyphic signs on a variety of surfaces. One surface was papyrus, an early kind of paper.

If you were a student who finished scribal school, you could get a good job in ancient Egypt. You might become a doctor or a priest, the secretary to a noble family, or the manager of a group of workers. Jobs that required the ability to read and write were desired, and young scribes worked hard; they knew that a good education meant a good life.

Exercise 7 · Blueprint for Writing: Outline

_____

I. _____

    A. _____

    B. _____

    C. _____

    D. _____

II. _____

    A. _____

    B. _____

    C. _____

    D. _____

III. _____

    A. _____

    B. _____

    C. _____

    D. _____

IV. _____

    A. _____

    B. _____

    C. _____

    D. _____

_____

Exercise 8 · Write It: Introductory Paragraph

▸ Read the topic sentence.

▸ Paraphrase the main ideas from the **Blueprint for Writing: Outline** to add to the introductory paragraph frame.

▸ Read the entire paragraph.

In ancient Egypt, going to scribal school provided an opportunity for a good future. Many children were not _____. The complicated Egyptian language _____. Students learned about _____. Those who finished scribal school _____. It was worth all the effort to become a scribe!

Exercise 1 · Listening for Stressed Syllables

▸ Listen to each word your teacher says. Repeat the word.

▸ Count the syllables. Write the number in the first column.

▸ Listen as your teacher says the word again. Identify the stressed syllable.

▸ Write the letters for the stressed syllable in the correct column.

	How many syllables do you hear?	First Syllable	Second Syllable	Third Syllable
1.				
2.				
3.				
4.				
5.				

Exercise 2 · Sort It: Meaning Categories

▸ Read the words in the **Word Bank**.

▸ Sort the words into categories according to meaning.

▸ Use the text selections **"Living in Egypt"** and **"Growing Up Egyptian"** for context clues about word meaning as needed.

▸ Write the words in the correct columns.

Word Bank

Nile River	Hebeny	Thebes	scribe	Egypt
Moses	Memphis	father	September	farmer
ancient	today	June	Africa	

People	Places	Time

Exercise 3 · Write It: Multiparagraph Composition

▸ Rewrite your introductory paragraph from Lesson 9, Exercise 8.

▸ Use your **Blueprint for Writing: Outline** to write the first body paragraph with your teacher.

▸ Finish writing the composition on your own.

▸ Read the entire composition, including the conclusion provided on the next page.

Introduction

_____

_____

_____

_____

_____

_____

(continued)

Exercise 3 (continued) · Write It: Multiparagraph Composition

Body 1
_____
_____
_____
_____

Body 2
_____
_____
_____
_____

Body 3
_____
_____
_____
_____

Body 4
_____
_____
_____
_____

Conclusion
    In ancient Egypt, receiving an education as a scribe was one way to be successful. Although there were many challenges, a good education was well worth the effort.

Check off the activities you complete with each lesson. Evaluate your accomplishments at the end of each lesson. Pay attention to teacher evaluations and comments.

Unit Objectives	Lesson 1 (Date:_____)	Lesson 2 (Date:_____)
STEP 1 — Phonemic Awareness and Phonics • Segment syllables from multisyllable words. • Identify syllable types: closed, r-controlled, open, and final silent e syllables. • Identify stressed syllables.		
STEP 2 — Word Recognition and Spelling • Read and spell multisyllable words. • Read and spell Essential Words. • Read and spell words with prefixes and suffixes. • Read and spell compound words.	❑ Exercise 1: Spelling Pretest 1 ❑ Exercise 2: Sentence Dictation	❑ Exercise 1: Sort It: Syllable Types ❑ Exercise 2: Build It ❑ Exercise 3: Sentence Dictation ❑ Word Fluency 1 ❑ Handwriting Practice
STEP 3 — Vocabulary and Morphology • Identify noun and adjective suffixes. • Identify antonyms, synonyms, and word attributes. • Use the meaning of prefixes to define words.	❑ Unit Vocabulary ❑ Explore It (T) ❑ Expression of the Day	❑ Exercise 4: Identify It: Noun Suffixes ❑ Exercise 5: Identify It: Adjective Suffixes ❑ Expression of the Day
STEP 4 — Grammar and Usage • Identify noun functions. • Identify main verbs and helping verbs. • Identify irregular verbs. • Identify and write compound sentences.	❑ Exercise 3: Sort It: Noun Categories ❑ Exercise 4: Identify It: Noun Functions	❑ Exercise 6: Code It: Noun Functions
STEP 5 — Listening and Reading Comprehension • Use context-based strategies to define words. • Identify topic, main ideas, and details. • Answer questions that use different types of signal words.	❑ Exercise 5: Phrase It ❑ Independent Text: "Life at the Pole"	❑ Passage Fluency 1 ❑ Exercise 7: Use the Clues
STEP 6 — Speaking and Writing • Organize main ideas and details for writing. • Create an outline to write a multiparagraph composition. • Use transition words for classification paragraphs.	❑ Masterpiece Sentences: Stages 1–3	❑ Exercise 8: Rewrite It: Pronouns
Self-Evaluation (5 is the highest) **Effort** = I produced my best work. **Participation** = I was actively involved in tasks. **Independence** = I worked on my own.	**Effort:** 1 2 3 4 5 **Participation:** 1 2 3 4 5 **Independence:** 1 2 3 4 5	**Effort:** 1 2 3 4 5 **Participation:** 1 2 3 4 5 **Independence:** 1 2 3 4 5
Teacher Evaluation	**Effort:** 1 2 3 4 5 **Participation:** 1 2 3 4 5 **Independence:** 1 2 3 4 5	**Effort:** 1 2 3 4 5 **Participation:** 1 2 3 4 5 **Independence:** 1 2 3 4 5

Lesson 3 (Date:_____)	Lesson 4 (Date:_____)	Lesson 5 (Date:_____)
❑ Exercise 1: Sort It: Syllable Types ❑ Exercise 2: Build It ❑ Exercise 3: Sentence Dictation ❑ Word Fluency 1	❑ Exercise 1: Sort It: Syllable Types ❑ Exercise 2: Build It ❑ Exercise 3: Sentence Dictation ❑ Word Fluency 2	❑ Content Mastery: Spelling Posttest 1
❑ Exercise 4: Word Networks: Synonyms ❑ Draw It: Idioms ❑ Expression of the Day	❑ Exercise 4: Match It: Using Prefixes ❑ Exercise 5: Rewrite It: Verb Tenses ❑ Expression of the Day	❑ Multiple Meaning Map (T) ❑ Draw It: Idioms ❑ Expression of the Day
❑ Exercise 5: Identify It: Main or Helping Verb ❑ Exercise 6: Choose It and Use It: The Verbs **be**, **have**, and **do**	❑ Exercise 6: Find It: Irregular Verb Forms ❑ Exercise 7: Rewrite It: Irregular Past Tense	❑ Masterpiece Sentences: All Stages
❑ Instructional Text: "Mysteries of Antarctica" ❑ Exercise 7: Use the Clues	❑ Exercise 8: Blueprint for Reading: Identifying Topic Sentence, Main Ideas, and Details (T)	❑ Exercise 1: Analyzing a Writing Sample (T)
❑ Exercise 8: Answer It	❑ Exercise 9: Blueprint for Writing: Outline (T) ❑ Challenge Text: "Continental Drift"	❑ Analyzing the Body Paragraphs of a Writing Sample (T) ❑ Challenge Text: "Continental Drift"
Effort: 1 2 3 4 5 **Participation:** 1 2 3 4 5 **Independence:** 1 2 3 4 5	**Effort:** 1 2 3 4 5 **Participation:** 1 2 3 4 5 **Independence:** 1 2 3 4 5	**Effort:** 1 2 3 4 5 **Participation:** 1 2 3 4 5 **Independence:** 1 2 3 4 5
Effort: 1 2 3 4 5 **Participation:** 1 2 3 4 5 **Independence:** 1 2 3 4 5	**Effort:** 1 2 3 4 5 **Participation:** 1 2 3 4 5 **Independence:** 1 2 3 4 5	**Effort:** 1 2 3 4 5 **Participation:** 1 2 3 4 5 **Independence:** 1 2 3 4 5

Check off the activities you complete with each lesson. Evaluate your accomplishments at the end of each lesson. Pay attention to teacher evaluations and comments.

Unit Objectives	Lesson 6 (Date:_____)	Lesson 7 (Date:_____)
STEP 1 **Phonemic Awareness and Phonics** • Segment syllables from multisyllable words. • Identify syllable types: **closed**, **r-controlled**, **open**, and **final silent e** syllables. • Identify stressed syllables.	❑ Exercise 1: Syllable Awareness: Segmentation	❑ Exercise 1: Listening for Stressed Syllables
STEP 2 **Word Recognition and Spelling** • Read and spell multisyllable words. • Read and spell **Essential Words**. • Read and spell words with prefixes and suffixes. • Read and spell compound words.	❑ Exercise 2: Spelling Pretest 2 ❑ Exercise 3: Sort It: Compound Words ❑ Word Fluency 3	❑ Exercise 2: Divide It ❑ Word Fluency 4
STEP 3 **Vocabulary and Morphology** • Identify noun and adjective suffixes. • Identify antonyms, synonyms, and word attributes. • Use the meaning of prefixes to define words.	❑ Exercise 4: Identify It: Present and Past Participles ❑ Exercise 5: Rewrite It: Present and Past Participles ❑ Expression of the Day	❑ Exercise 3: Match It: Prefixes ❑ Expression of the Day
STEP 4 **Grammar and Usage** • Identify noun functions. • Identify main verbs and helping verbs. • Identify irregular verbs. • Identify and write compound sentences.	❑ Exercise 6: Find It: Compound Sentences ❑ Exercise 7: Combine It: Compound Sentences	❑ Exercise 4: Diagram It: Compound Sentences (T)
STEP 5 **Listening and Reading Comprehension** • Use context-based strategies to define words. • Identify topic, main ideas, and details. • Answer questions that use different types of signal words.	❑ Instructional Text: "The First Transcontinental Railroad" (T) ❑ Exercise 8: Use the Clues	❑ Exercise 5: Blueprint for Reading: Main Ideas (T)
STEP 6 **Speaking and Writing** • Organize main ideas and details for writing. • Create an outline to write a multiparagraph composition. • Use transition words for classification paragraphs.	❑ Exercise 9: Answer It	❑ Exercise 6: Blueprint for Writing: Outline (T) ❑ Exercise 7: Write It: Introductory Paragraph ❑ Challenge Text: "The Quest for a Continent"
Self-Evaluation (5 is the highest) **Effort** = I produced my best work. **Participation** = I was actively involved in tasks. **Independence** = I worked on my own.	**Effort:** 1 2 3 4 5 **Participation:** 1 2 3 4 5 **Independence:** 1 2 3 4 5	**Effort:** 1 2 3 4 5 **Participation:** 1 2 3 4 5 **Independence:** 1 2 3 4 5
Teacher Evaluation	**Effort:** 1 2 3 4 5 **Participation:** 1 2 3 4 5 **Independence:** 1 2 3 4 5	**Effort:** 1 2 3 4 5 **Participation:** 1 2 3 4 5 **Independence:** 1 2 3 4 5

Lesson 8 (Date:_____)	Lesson 9 (Date:_____)	Lesson 10 (Date:_____)
		❑ Summative Test: Phonemic Awareness and Phonics
❑ Progress Indicators: Test of Silent Word Reading Fluency (TOSWRF)	❑ Progress Indicators: Spelling Inventory	❑ Content Mastery: Spelling Posttest 2
❑ Exercise 1: Word Networks: Analogies ❑ Exercise 2: Word Networks: Word Pairs With Prefixes ❑ Expression of the Day	❑ Exercise 1: Find It: Word Forms ❑ Exercise 2: Choose It and Use It: Prefixes ❑ Expression of the Day	❑ Summative Test: Vocabulary and Morphology
❑ Masterpiece Sentences: Compound Sentences	❑ Exercise 3: Rewrite It: Compound Sentences	❑ Summative Test: Grammar and Usage
❑ Blueprint for Reading: Details (T)		❑ Progress Indicators: Degrees of Reading Power (DRP)
❑ Blueprint for Writing: Outline (T) ❑ Writing a Multiparagraph Composition: Writing Body Paragraphs ❑ Challenge Text: "The Quest for a Continent"	❑ Summative Test: Composition	

Effort: 1 2 3 4 5 **Participation:** 1 2 3 4 5 **Independence:** 1 2 3 4 5	**Effort:** 1 2 3 4 5 **Participation:** 1 2 3 4 5 **Independence:** 1 2 3 4 5	**Effort:** 1 2 3 4 5 **Participation:** 1 2 3 4 5 **Independence:** 1 2 3 4 5
Effort: 1 2 3 4 5 **Participation:** 1 2 3 4 5 **Independence:** 1 2 3 4 5	**Effort:** 1 2 3 4 5 **Participation:** 1 2 3 4 5 **Independence:** 1 2 3 4 5	**Effort:** 1 2 3 4 5 **Participation:** 1 2 3 4 5 **Independence:** 1 2 3 4 5

Exercise 1 · Spelling Pretest 1

▶ Write the words your teacher says.

1. _____   6. _____   11. _____

2. _____   7. _____   12. _____

3. _____   8. _____   13. _____

4. _____   9. _____   14. _____

5. _____   10. _____   15. _____

Exercise 2 · Sentence Dictation

▸ Listen to each sentence your teacher says.

▸ Repeat the sentence.

▸ Write it on the line.

▸ Check for sentence signals—capital letters and end punctuation.

1. _____

2. _____

3. _____

4. _____

5. _____

▸ Read the dictated sentences 1–5.

▸ Find the three words that follow the **Doubling Rule**.

▸ Write those three words on the lines.

_____   _____   _____

Exercise 3 · Sort It: Noun Categories

▶ Preview the four categories in the chart below (people, places, things, ideas).

▶ Read the nouns in the **Word Bank**.

▶ Write each noun in the appropriate column.

▶ Review your nouns with your teacher to ensure that they are in the right columns.

Word Bank

scientists	climate	krill	zone
brine	researcher	South Pole	worker
seeds	winter	Antarctica	fossils
mass	shore	engineer	past
ocean	weather	explorer	month

People	Places	Things	Ideas

Exercise 4 · Identify It: Noun Functions

▶ Read each sentence and study the underlined noun.

▶ Decide if the noun is the **subject, direct object, indirect object** or **object of a preposition**.

▶ Fill in the correct bubble.

▶ Do the first sentence with your teacher.

	Subject	Direct Object	Indirect Object	Object of a Preposition
1. The South Pole is on <u>Antarctica</u>.	○	○	○	○
2. <u>Antarctica</u> is the frozen continent.	○	○	○	○
3. Small plants live on the frozen <u>shore</u>.	○	○	○	○
4. Whales migrate and eat <u>krill</u>.	○	○	○	○
5. Scientists gave <u>whales</u> krill.	○	○	○	○
6. The migrating birds bring <u>seeds</u>.	○	○	○	○
7. Antarctica can offer <u>us</u> new information.	○	○	○	○
8. <u>Scientists</u> establish labs in Antarctica.	○	○	○	○
9. Antarctica was part of the original land <u>mass</u>.	○	○	○	○
10. <u>Fossils</u> have been found in Antarctica.	○	○	○	○

Exercise 5 · Phrase It

▸ Use the penciling strategy to "scoop" the phrases in each sentence.

▸ Read them as you would speak them.

▸ The first two are done for you.

1. The temperature is less than zero.

2. The wind chill hits the danger zone.

3. It is very dry and cold in Antarctica.

4. Small plants live on the frozen shore.

5. Summer begins in October and ends in March.

6. A few months pass, and the planet tilts.

7. Winter is dark all the time.

8. There is some light in the sky.

9. Light comes from gases.

10. Swirling gases color the sky.

Exercise 1 · Sort It: Syllable Types

▸ Read the syllables in the **Word Bank**.

▸ Sort the syllables by syllable type.

▸ Write each syllable in the appropriate column.

Word Bank

mar	ket
der	er
pet	un
port	trans
stand	car

Closed	r-Controlled

Unit 18 · Lesson 2

Exercise 2 · Build It

▸ Combine syllables from Exercise 1, **Sort It: Syllable Types**, to build five new words in three minutes.

▸ Write the words on the lines.

▸ Read and compare words with a partner.

_____   _____   _____

_____   _____   _____

Exercise 3 · Sentence Dictation

▸ Listen to each sentence your teacher says.

▸ Repeat the sentence.

▸ Write it on the line.

▸ Check for sentence signals—capital letters and end punctuation.

1. _____

2. _____

3. _____

4. _____

5. _____

▸ Read the dictated sentences 1–5.

▸ Which three words or phrases answer the question "When?"

▸ Write those three words or phrases on the lines.

_____   _____   _____

Exercise 4 · Identify It: Noun Suffixes

▸ Read each sentence.

▸ Make an **X** in the column to identify if the underlined word is:
  A singular noun (just one)
  A plural noun (two or more)
  A singular possessive noun (just one owner)
  A plural possessive noun (two or more owners)

▸ Work through the examples with your teacher.

Sentence	Singular Noun	Plural Noun	Singular Possessive	Plural Possessive
Examples: In 1498, the explorer Vasco De Gama discovered a new type of <u>bird</u>.	X			
<u>Flocks</u> of these birds jumped in and out of the water and did not fly.		X		
Never before had Vasco <u>De Gama's</u> men observed an odd looking animal.			X	
The <u>birds'</u> shapes were like bowling pins on two webbed feet.				X
1. A penguin has a black <u>back</u> and a white front.				
2. Penguins walk clumsily but swim briskly, using their wings and feet like <u>flippers</u>.				
3. They make <u>nests</u> on land.				
4. They eat fish and <u>squid</u>.				
5. <u>Penguins'</u> lives have some fun.				

(continued)

Exercise 4 (continued) · Identify It: Noun Suffixes

Sentence	Singular Noun	Plural Noun	Singular Possessive	Plural Possessive
6. After all, they get to slide on <u>patches</u> of snow and ice into the water.				
7. Like every bird, a penguin's life begins in an <u>egg</u>.				
8. The <u>birds</u>' eggs are often laid in sets of two.				
9. If the weather gets too cold, the mother hides the eggs in a fold of skin that stretches over the <u>mother's</u> stomach.				
10. After the <u>chicks</u> hatch, both parents feed them.				

Exercise 5 · Identify It: Adjective Suffixes

▶ Read each sentence.

▶ Make an X in the column to show if the underlined word is:
A comparative adjective (compares two nouns or pronouns)
A superlative adjective (compares three or more nouns or pronouns)
An adverb formed from an adjective (often answers the questions *how* or *when*)

Sentences	Comparative Adjective	Superlative Adjective	Adverb from Adjective
Examples: Sharks <u>easily</u> catch young penguin chicks.			X
Penguins are the <u>funniest</u> birds you have ever seen.		X	
The absurd-looking bird has an even <u>sillier</u> call; it sounds like a mule or a donkey.	X		
1. On land they appear to be one of the <u>clumsiest</u> animals alive.			
2. In the water they are <u>sleeker</u> than many fish.			
3. Dinners of raw fish and squid do not <u>exactly</u> help penguins to smell like roses.			
4. People would think you were <u>smellier</u> than a skunk if you tried to live and eat like this bird.			
5. In fact, some people say penguins are the <u>smelliest</u> birds of all.			
6. Other people say that they are <u>funnier</u> than any other animal.			
7. Many people <u>really</u> like watching penguins at the zoo.			

(continued)

Exercise 5 *(continued)* · **Identify It: Adjective Suffixes**

Sentences	Comparative Adjective	Superlative Adjective	Adverb from Adjective
8. <u>Fewer</u> people, however, like the smell of these birds.			
9. Whales migrate to the <u>coldest</u> continent for krill.			
10. Their winter is <u>darker</u> than ours.			

Exercise 6 · Code It: Noun Functions

▸ Read the text.

▸ Decide if each underlined noun is a **subject,** a **direct object,** or an **object of a preposition**.

▸ Write **s** above each subject, **DO** above each direct object, and **OP** above each object of a preposition.

▸ Do the first example with your teacher.

---

from "Life at the Pole"

In the <u>summer</u> at the <u>South Pole</u>, <u>days</u> are long. It is never dark.

Thick <u>shades</u> on <u>homes</u> block the <u>sun</u>. These make the <u>rooms</u> dark.

<u>People</u> can then sleep. After a few <u>months</u>, the <u>planet</u> tilts. <u>Winter</u>

starts. Only swirling <u>gases</u> light the <u>sky</u>.

Unit 18 · Lesson 2

Exercise 7 · Use the Clues

▸ Read each pair of sentences.

▸ Find each circled pronoun.

▸ Identify the noun that the pronoun replaces.

▸ Underline the noun that the pronoun replaces.

▸ Draw an arrow to show the link between the pronoun and the noun it replaces.

1. There is some light in the sky. (It) comes from gases.

2. Shades block the sun. (They) make sleep possible.

3. Many countries govern Antarctica. People go (there) to study.

4. People go there to study. (They) want to understand the planet better.

5. This land was not always frozen. At one time (it) was part of a lush forest.

Exercise 8 · Rewrite It: Pronouns

▸ Reread each sentence pair in Exercise 7, **Use the Clues**.

▸ Replace the circled pronoun with the noun that it represents.

▸ Rewrite the sentence using the noun.

▸ Read the new sentence.

▸ Check for sentence signals—capital letters, commas, and end punctuation.

1. _____

2. _____

3. _____

4. _____

5. _____

Exercise 1 · Sort It: Syllable Types

▶ Read the syllables in the **Word Bank**.

▶ Sort the syllables by syllable type.

▶ Write each syllable in the correct column.

Word Bank

do	tor	er	pre	pen
u	o	vent	na	men

Closed	r-Controlled	Open

Exercise 2 · Build It

▸ Combine syllables from Exercise 1, **Sort It: Syllable Types**, to build five new words in three minutes.

▸ Write the words on the lines.

▸ Read and compare words with a partner.

_____   _____   _____

_____   _____

Exercise 3 · Sentence Dictation

▸ Listen to each sentence your teacher says.

▸ Repeat the sentence.

▸ Write it on the line.

▸ Check for sentence signals—capital letters and end punctuation.

1. _____

2. _____

3. _____

4. _____

5. _____

▸ Read the dictated sentences 1–5.

▸ Which two words follow the **Change It Rule**?

▸ Write those two words on the lines.

_____   _____

Unit 18 · Lesson 3

Exercise 4 · Word Networks: Synonyms

▸ Read the paragraph.

▸ Replace each underlined word with a synonym.

▸ Write the synonyms on the lines below.

▸ Use a dictionary or thesaurus for extra help.

▸ Reread the paragraph with the new words.

---

adapted from "Life at the Pole"

The temperature is less than zero! The wind <u>gusts</u> at more than 200 miles
per hour. The wind chill <u>hits</u> the danger zone. The <u>land</u> is frozen. Welcome
to Antarctica. Small plants live on the frozen shore. <u>Krill</u> thrive in the cold
waters. Whales <u>migrate</u> to the Antarctic. Many birds visit too.

---

1. gusts: _____

2. hits: _____

3. land: _____

4. krill: _____

5. migrate: _____

Exercise 5 · Identify It: Main or Helping Verb

▸ Read each sentence.

▸ Underline the verb or verb phrase in each sentence.

▸ Decide if **be**, **have**, or **do** is used as a main verb or a helping verb.

▸ Fill in the correct bubble.

▸ Do the first sentence with your teacher.

	Main Verb	Helping Verb
1. The sun has set over the frozen land.	○	○
2. The seawater is cold.	○	○
3. Large icebergs have formed in the sea.	○	○
4. Scientists will be studying the diverse plants.	○	○
5. Some plants do live on the frozen shore.	○	○
6. The penguins were on the iceberg.	○	○
7. Whales will be looking for krill next summer.	○	○
8. The scientists did many tests in their labs.	○	○
9. The long winter has brought dark days and nights.	○	○
10. Different animals are out on the icebergs.	○	○

Exercise 6 · Choose It and Use It: The Verbs Be, Have, and Do

▸ Read each sentence.

▸ Choose the correct form of the verb from the helping verb chart in the *Student Text*, page 242.

▸ Fill in the blank with the correct form of the verb.

▸ Do the first sentence with your teacher.

1. Yesterday, the sun _____ rise for the first time this summer.
   to do

2. Next summer the whales _____ returning to Antarctica.
   to be

3. Scientists _____ studied the plant life of this frozen zone.
   to have

4. Penguins _____ strange black and white birds.
   to be

5. Whales _____ two large flukes dividing their tails.
   to have

Exercise 7 · Use the Clues

‣ Use context clues to define **aurora**.

‣ Underline the vocabulary word.

‣ Read text before and after the unknown word.

‣ Highlight the text that helps to define **aurora**.

> **from "Mysteries of Antarctica"**
>
> In Antarctica, the seasons are different. They are reversed from the Northern Hemisphere. Summer lasts from October to March. Winter lasts from April to September. In the summer, daylight lasts 24 hours a day. In winter, it stays dark all day. During the dark winter months, there is often an aurora display. Green, orange, and red clouds of gas flash across the sky.

Define It

‣ Write a definition based on the context clues.

‣ Verify your definition with the dictionary or www.yourdictionary.com.

aurora— _____

_____

_____

Unit 18 · Lesson 3

Exercise 8 · Answer It

▸ Underline the signal word in each question.

▸ Answer the questions in complete sentences.

▸ Check for sentence signals—capital letters, commas, and end punctuation.

1. Explain why Antarctica is considered a mysterious continent.

_____

_____

_____

_____

2. Distinguish between the seasons in Antarctica and your hometown.

_____

_____

_____

_____

3. Categorize the jobs of a scientist working in Antarctica.

_____

_____

_____

_____

(continued)

Exercise 8 (continued) · **Answer It**

4. Explain why scientists search for meteorites in Antarctica.

_____

_____

_____

_____

5. Was Antarctica ever connected to other continents? Explain. Is it connected now? Explain.

_____

_____

_____

_____

Exercise 1 · Sort It: Syllable Types

▸ Read the syllables in the **Word Bank**.

▸ Sort the syllables by syllable type.

▸ Write each syllable in the correct column.

Word Bank

fe	base	line	fume	ver
per	flate	sis	in	ter

Closed	r-Controlled	Open	Final Silent e

Exercise 2 · Build It

▶ Combine syllables from Exercise 1, **Sort It: Syllable Types,** to build five new words in three minutes.

▶ Write the words on the lines.

▶ Read and compare words with a partner.

_____   _____   _____

_____   _____   _____

Exercise 3 · Sentence Dictation

▶ Listen to each sentence your teacher says.

▶ Repeat the sentence.

▶ Write it on the line.

▶ Check for sentence signals—capital letters, commas, and end punctuation.

1. _____

2. _____

3. _____

4. _____

5. _____

▶ Read the dictated sentences 1–5.

▶ Which three words follow the **Drop e Rule**?

▶ Write those three words on the lines.

_____   _____   _____

Unit 18 · Lesson 4

Exercise 4 · Match It: Using Prefixes

▶ Use what you know about the prefixes to match each word with the definition of its prefix.

▶ Draw a line to match the word with its definition.

▶ Use a dictionary to verify answers.

Word	Definition
1. indoors	**a.** not
2. distrust	**b.** below
3. underwater	**c.** between, among
4. nonsense	**d.** into
5. interstate	**e.** away, apart

▶ Use the words with prefixes to complete these activities.

▶ Complete the sentences:

    1. A large road that goes between states is a(n) _____ .

    2. The opposite of being above water is _____ .

▶ Complete the antonym pairs:

    1. sense: _____

    2. outdoors: _____

    3. trust: _____

Exercise 5 · Rewrite It: Verb Tenses

▸ Review the **Tense Timeline** with your teacher.

Past	Present	Future
Yesterday	Today	Tomorrow

▸ Use suffixes to change the verb to the indicated tense. Write the verb in the blank.

▸ Use the **Doubling** and **Drop e Rules** when necessary.

▸ Read the sentence quietly to check your work.

Base Verb	Tense	Sentence
Examples		
glide	present progressive	Christopher Columbus and his men **are gliding** in three ships to the continent, America.
help	past	The King and Queen of Spain **helped** Columbus pay for the three ships.
enter	present	Columbus **enters** an unexplored part of the sea.
1. spot	present	When a sailor _____ a pelican he shouts out with joy.
2. say	present progressive	Columbus _____ that pelicans mean land is nearby.
3. pluck	future	A few days later they _____ a branch from the water.
4. land	past	At two o'clock in the morning, October 12, 1492, they _____ on a small island.
5. swim	present progressive	The next day, people _____ to the boat to bring gifts to Columbus and his men.

Unit 18 · Lesson 4

Exercise 6 · Find It: Irregular Verb Forms

▸ Read each sentence.

▸ Underline the past tense verb.

▸ Write the past, present, and future forms of the verb in the chart below the **Tense Timeline**.

1. The storm clouds flew overhead.

2. During the summer the days became very long.

3. Scientists did all their work out on the icebergs.

4. The sun began to sink below the horizon.

5. During the winter, the whales went north to warmer waters.

6. The buildings withstood the strong winds.

7. In the dark, the men mistook the different machines.

8. Scientists brought all their equipment to Antarctica.

9. The frozen land shone in the sun.

10. Once Antarctica had abundant life and plants on it.

(continued)

Exercise 6 (continued) · Find It: Irregular Verb Forms

	Past	Present	Future
	Yesterday	Today	Tomorrow
	Irregular Past Tense	**Present Tense**	**Future Tense**
1.			
2.			
3.			
4.			
5.			
6.			
7.			
8.			
9.			
10.			

Exercise 7 • Rewrite It: Irregular Past Tense

▸ Read each sentence.

▸ Underline the verb.

▸ Rewrite the sentence, putting the verb into the past tense.

▸ Check for sentence signals—capital letters, commas, and end punctuation.

▸ Do the first sentence with your teacher.

1. The scientists lend their equipment to each other.

_____

_____

2. The experiment begins in the lab.

_____

_____

3. The iceberg becomes separated from the main pack.

_____

_____

4. In winter the birds fly north to warmer land.

_____

_____

5. During the winter the scientists do their work indoors.

_____

_____

Exercise 8 · Blueprint for Reading: Identifying Topic Sentence, Main Ideas, and Details

▸ Underline the topic sentence in the first paragraph.

▸ Use blue to highlight the main ideas in the second, third, and fourth paragraphs.

▸ Use pink to highlight the details in the second, third, and fourth paragraphs.

from "Mysteries of Antarctica"

Antarctica is a mysterious continent. Some call it a penguin's playground. Others call it the end of the Earth. Antarctica is the home of the South Pole. Want to visit the South Pole? There, you can "walk around the world" in a few steps. You can step on every time zone and longitude in less than a minute. Check for yourself. Look at Antarctica on a globe.

In Antarctica, the seasons are different. They are reversed. Summer lasts from October to March. Winter lasts from April to September. In the summer, daylight lasts 24 hours a day. In winter, it stays dark all day. During the dark winter months, there is often an aurora display. Green, orange, and red clouds of gas flash across the sky.

The weather in Antarctica is very dry, cold, and windy. It has the harshest climate of all the continents. It has only about three inches of snowfall each year. Antarctica has been called the frozen frontier. Just how cold is it? It's never above freezing. Only a small amount

(continued)

of the land is free from ice. Antarctica's glaciers hold about three-fourths of all the fresh water on Earth. Icebergs break off from the ice shelves. Some are larger than the big island of Hawaii. The winds are very strong. They are called the katabatics. These heavy winds blow up to 200 miles per hour. The windchill factor is very low. Diane Di Massa is an oceanographic engineer. She says, "This makes it difficult and dangerous to do research here."

Even with the harsh weather, plants and animals can survive in Antarctica. It is home to some very small life forms. Algae live along the coastlines. They live inside sea ice. They survive in salty brine channels during the dark winter. In springtime, when sea ice melts, they flow into the ocean. These cells need sunlight and carbon dioxide to grow. This is the basis of an important food chain. Next on the food chain are krill. Krill look like small red shrimp. They are a favorite food of Earth's largest mammal, the endangered blue whale. Blue whales migrate to the southern oceans to eat this rich food. Other animals visit Antarctica, too. They include penguins, seabirds, seals, and other types of whales.

Exercise 9 · Blueprint for Writing: Outline

▸ Use the highlighted text from Exercise 8, **Blueprint for Reading: Identifying Topic Sentence, Main Ideas, and Details** to complete the **Blueprint for Writing: Outline**.

▸ Add transition words to the outline by drawing circles in the margins next to the main ideas. Write the transition words inside the circles.

_____

I. _____

   A. _____

   B. _____

   C. _____

   D. _____

II. _____

   A. _____

   B. _____

   C. _____

   D. _____

III. _____

   A. _____

   B. _____

   C. _____

   D. _____

Exercise 1 · Analyzing a Writing Sample

▶ Read the introductory paragraph with your teacher.

▶ Underline the topic in the first paragraph.

▶ Highlight the main ideas in the first paragraph in blue.

▶ With your teacher, discuss the link between the paraphrased main ideas in the introductory paragraph and those on the **Blueprint for Writing: Outline** from Lesson 4, Exercise 9.

---

from "Mysteries of Antarctica"

Antarctica is an extraordinary continent. The seasons are unlike those of other continents. The harsh weather is dry, cold and blustery. Few plants and animals can live in the severe conditions. Antarctica is a mysterious place for many reasons.

First of all, the seasons are unique. Summer lasts from October to March. The winter months are from April to May. It is daylight all summer and dark all winter.

In addition, the weather is harsh. Annually, the snowfall is only three inches, but the temperature is always below freezing. Forceful winds blow persistently.

Finally, some plants and animals can live in these difficult circumstances. Algae exist along the seashore. Whales feed on krill, which look like little red shrimp. Penguins, seabirds, and seals also survive in these conditions.

Exercise 1 · Syllable Awareness: Segmentation

▸ Listen to the word.

▸ Count the syllables. Write the number in the first column.

▸ Write the letter for each vowel sound you hear.

▸ Mark the vowel with a diacritical mark.

	How many syllables do you hear?	First vowel sound	Second vowel sound	Third vowel sound
1.				
2.				
3.				
4.				
5.				
6.				
7.				
8.				
9.				
10.				

Unit 18 · Lesson 6

Exercise 2 · Spelling Pretest 2

▸ Write the words your teacher says.

1. _____

2. _____

3. _____

4. _____

5. _____

6. _____

7. _____

8. _____

9. _____

10. _____

11. _____

12. _____

13. _____

14. _____

15. _____

Exercise 3 · Sort It: Compound Words

▸ Sort the words into categories.

▸ Record words on the chart.

Word Bank

brother	dateline	clockwork	exploring	tornado
outside	pathway	sunset	translate	antilock

Compound Words	Not Compound Words

Unit 18 · Lesson 6

Exercise 4 · Identify It: Present and Past Participles

▶ Read each phrase below.

▶ Underline the participle.

▶ Put an X in the correct column to show if the phrase contains a present participle or a past participle.

Phrase	Phrase Contains Present Participle	Phrase Contains Past Participle
1. An exciting ride		
2. A respected woman explorer		
3. A well-prepared meal		
4. Buzzing insects		
5. An unexplored land		
6. the connecting landmasses		
7. working parents		
8. explored territory		
9. crossing a continent		
10. an extended offer		

Exercise 5 · Rewrite It: Present and Past Participles

▶ Change the verb to the participle that best fits the meaning of the sentence.

▶ Read the sentences quietly to check your work.

Verb	Sentence
Examples: complete	The ___completed___ railroad connected the East and West Coasts.
laugh	A happy, ___laughing___ crowd gathered to witness the event.
1. excite	The _____ children ran back and forth.
2. swing	_____ hammers struck hot metal.
3. yell	_____ reporters pushed themselves to the front of the crowd.
4. dedicate	The _____ workers had constructed long lines of track across America.
5. finish	The _____ railroad would connect both sides of the continent.

Exercise 6 · Find It: Compound Sentences

▸ Read each compound sentence.

▸ Find the two complete sentences in each compound sentence and underline them.

▸ Circle the conjunction.

1. Scientists have found fossils, and even bits of Mars have been found.

2. Antarctica is now a frozen land, but at one time it was a lush forest.

3. Scientists can work outdoors, or they can work in the lab.

4. Many countries govern Antarctica, and it does not belong to any nation.

5. The winter nights are cold and dark, but the summer days are sunny and long.

Exercise 7 · Combine It: Compound Sentences

▸ Read each sentence pair.

▸ Decide whether to use the conjunction **and**, **but**, or **or** to join the sentences.

▸ Write the new compound sentence on the line.

▸ Circle the conjunction you used to join the sentences.

▸ Check for sentence signals—capital letters, commas, and end punctuation.

1. Huge waves crashed onto the iceberg.
   The water froze instantly.

   _____

   _____

2. Scientists find the long Antarctic night challenging.
   They still continue with their work.

   _____

   _____

3. The whales should swim north at the end of the summer.
   They will be trapped in the ice.

   _____

   _____

4. It is hard to sleep in the daylight.
   Shades make the rooms dark.

   _____

   _____

5. Scientists set up labs on the frozen continent.
   They study the thinning ozone.

   _____

   _____

Unit 18 · Lesson 6

Exercise 8 · Use the Clues

▸ Use word substitution to define the word **stature**.

▸ Underline the vocabulary word.

▸ Look for the word that renames the vocabulary word and circle it.

> ### from "The First Transcontinental Railroad"
>
> In 1849, the Chinese came to California for gold. Immigration from China had brought many Chinese to the western United States. Many went to work for the railroad. They were smaller in stature. But everyone learned that their smaller size didn't matter. The Chinese roadbed was straighter, smoother, and longer than that of any other crew. The Chinese worked without stopping. Their cooks would come among them with steaming buckets of tea, hung from long rods across their shoulders. That was enough to get them through the day.

▸ Write a definition based on the context clues.

▸ Verify your definition with the dictionary or www.yourdictionary.com.

stature— _____

Exercise 9 · Answer It

▸ Underline the signal word in the question.

▸ Write the answer in complete sentences.

1. Distinguish between the different transportation problems encountered by both railroad companies.

   _____

   _____

   _____

   _____

   _____

   _____

2. Compare the Union Pacific Railroad workers and the Central Pacific Railroad workers.

   _____

   _____

   _____

   _____

   _____

   _____

3. Describe the living conditions for the railroad workers.

   _____

   _____

   _____

   _____

   _____

(continued)

Exercise 9 (continued) · Answer It

4. Why do you think the Chinese workers were left out of the photograph taken at the completion of the railroad?

_____

_____

_____

_____

_____

5. Compare the mood conveyed by the author in the first two paragraphs with the mood in the last paragraph.

_____

_____

_____

_____

_____

Exercise 1 · Listening for Stressed Syllables

▶ Listen to the word your teacher says.

▶ Repeat the word.

▶ Listen for the stressed, or accented, syllable.

▶ Put an X in the box to mark the position of the stressed syllable.

	First syllable	Second syllable	Third syllable
1. again			
2. tomorrow			
3. together			
4. alone			
5. certain			

Exercise 2 · Divide It

▶ Read the sentence silently.

▶ Use the steps of **Divide It** to break the boldface words into syllables.

▶ Blend the syllables together to read each word.

▶ After dividing, read the sentences to a partner.

Two **locomotives** idled on their tracks. Thousands **labored** to **connect** the tracks. What an **amazing** task!

locomotives   labored   connect   amazing

Unit 18 · Lesson 7

Exercise 3 · Match It: Prefixes

▸ Use what you know about the prefixes to match each word with the definition of its prefix.

▸ Draw a line to connect the prefixed word with the definition of the prefix.

▸ Use a dictionary to verify answers.

Words with Prefixes	Definitions of Prefixes
1. substandard	a. across, beyond
2. transport	b. below
3. preboard	c. before
4. antitoxin	d. with
5. concert	e. against

▸ Write a prefix or a word with a prefix to complete the sentences.

1. Families with small children can board the airplane before others; they

   _____ the plane.

2. After the snakebite, the child was given an _____ .

3. The band played well together and everyone enjoyed the wonderful

   _____ .

4. Planes were used to _____ their equipment to the Antarctic.

5. She didn't want to work for _____ pay.

Exercise 4 · Diagram It: Compound Sentences

▸ Read each sentence.

▸ Find the two complete sentences and underline them.

▸ Circle the conjunction.

▸ Diagram the sentence.

▸ Do the first example with your teacher.

1. Scientists study the ozone layer, and they conduct many experiments.

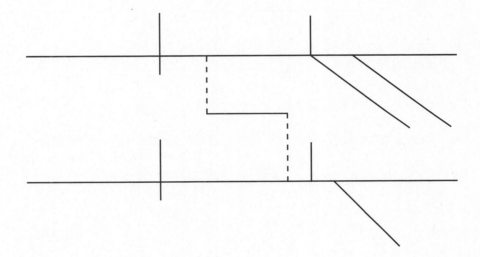

(continued)

Exercise 4 (continued) · Diagram It: Compound Sentences

2. Some ice melts at the South Pole, and the water level rises.

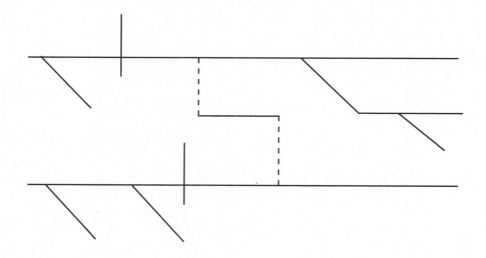

3. The penguins nest during the summer, but they leave the ice cap in winter.

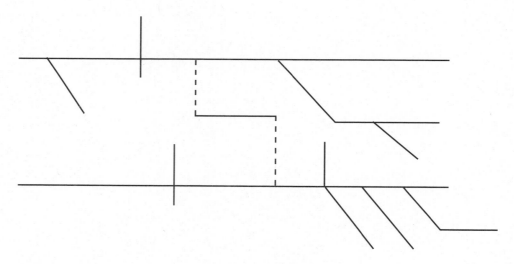

(continued)

Exercise 4 (continued) · **Diagram It: Compound Sentences**

4. The summer sun shines for long hours, but in winter the sun does not rise.

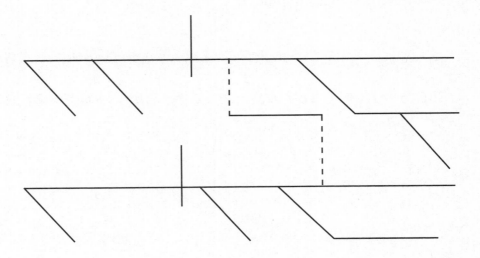

5. Scientists find fossils, and they learn details about earlier life.

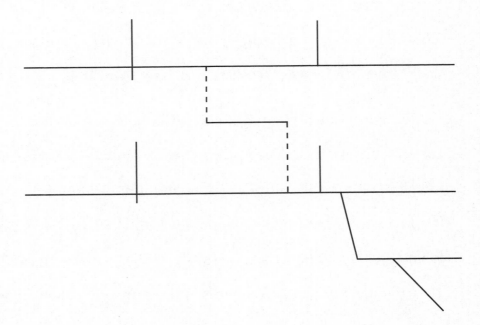

Exercise 5 · Blueprint for Reading: Main Ideas

▸ Listen to your teacher read this excerpt from **"The First Transcontinental Railroad."**

▸ Highlight the main ideas in blue.

---

from "The First Transcontinental Railroad"

From the East: The Workers of the Union Pacific Railroad

One group of workers was employed by the Union Pacific Railroad. This railroad company had already reached Omaha. Now, it was moving west across the continent. It had all the workers it could use. Twelve thousand men had drifted there from the North and the South. The Civil War was over. Privates, sergeants, lieutenants, captains, and colonels were unemployed. Soldiers from both sides needed work. Former slaves needed work. Ex-convicts needed work. The biggest group was the Irish. Many of them had fought in the war. Many others were fresh off the boat from Ireland.

Living conditions were difficult. The men lived in tents or in converted boxcars. Towns sprang up at the end of the line. These towns were portable. After about 50 miles of new track had been laid, the merchants and townspeople raced up the track to set up a new town. They took down their flimsy buildings, often with canvas roofs. They piled everything on wagons and set up again at the new spot.

(continued)

From the West: The Workers of the Central Pacific Railroad

Another group of workers was employed by the Central Pacific Railroad. This company was laying track from Sacramento, California. It would join the Union Pacific Railroad, which was crawling out from Omaha. The railroad bosses of the Central Pacific Railroad had a more difficult time finding reliable workers. Many would quit after a week or two. They worked only long enough to earn money. Then, they would go back to prospecting for gold.

In 1849, the Chinese came to California for gold. Immigration from China had brought many Chinese to the western United States. Many went to work for the railroad. They were smaller in stature. But everyone learned that their smaller size didn't matter. The Chinese roadbed was straighter, smoother, and longer than that of any other crew. The Chinese worked without stopping. Their cooks would walk among them with steaming buckets of tea, hung from long rods across their shoulders. That was enough to get them through the day.

Unit 18 · Lesson 7

Exercise 6 · Blueprint for Writing: Outline

▸ Listen to your teacher reread the introduction from **"The First Transcontinental Railroad."**

▸ Write the topic on the first line of the outline.

▸ Paraphrase the main ideas from Exercise 7 and write them on the outline.

_____

I. _____

    A. _____

    B. _____

    C. _____

    D. _____

II. _____

    A. _____

    B. _____

    C. _____

    D. _____

III. _____

    A. _____

    B. _____

    C. _____

    D. _____

(continued)

Exercise 6 (*continued*) · **Blueprint for Writing: Outline**

IV. _____

    A. _____

    B. _____

    C. _____

    D. _____

_____

Unit 18 · Lesson 7

Exercise 7 · Write It: Introductory Paragraph

▸ Listen to your teacher reread the introduction from **"The First Transcontinental Railroad."**

▸ Use the **Blueprint for Reading: Outline** for **"The First Transcontinental Railroad"** to write an introductory paragraph.

_____

_____

_____

_____

_____

_____

_____

_____

_____

_____

_____

_____

_____

_____

_____

_____

Exercise 1 · Word Networks: Analogies

▸ Read the first word pair.

▸ Identify the relationship between the words.

▸ Write another pair of words that shows that same relationship.

▸ Do the example with your teacher.

Examples: sunset: end

sunrise: beginning

1. eye: look
    _____

2. before: after
    _____

3. continent: land
    _____

4. locate: find
    _____

5. number: math
    _____

Exercise 2 · Word Networks: Word Pairs With Prefixes

▸ Read the word pairs.

▸ Think about the meaning of the prefix in both words.

▸ Fill in the bubble that matches the meaning of the prefix.

▸ Do the example together.

Example: Listen: **subway: submarine**

What does the prefix in this word pair mean?

subway: submarine

○ A. over

○ B. below

○ C. against

Fill in the bubble for **below**. The prefix **sub-** means **under** or **below**.

▸ Finish the remaining items independently.

1. **anti-drug: anti-war**

   ○ A. against

   ○ B. opposite

   ○ C. into

2. **predate: preshrunk**

   ○ A. with

   ○ B. across

   ○ C. before

3. **interact: interstate**

   ○ A. over

   ○ B. between

   ○ C. apart

4. **redo: refinish**

   ○ A. again

   ○ B. over

   ○ C. not

5. **unexplored: unopened**

   ○ A. again

   ○ B. over

   ○ C. not

Exercise 1 · Find It: Word Forms

▸ Read the word form.

▸ Read the sentence.

▸ Underline the word in the sentence that shows the form named in the first column.

▸ Do the examples with your teacher.

Form	Sentence
Examples: Singular possessive	Some people call the continent of Antarctica a penguin's playground.
Past participle	Others call it a frozen frontier of snow and ice.
3rd person singular present tense verb	In the center of the continent stands the South Pole.
Singular noun	It isn't a real pole, of course.
Adjective	The first person to reach the South Pole was the daring explorer Roald Amundsen.
1. Adverb made from adjective	On January 15, 1911, his men quickly began to set up a base camp on the continent of Antarctica.
2. Compound noun	Nine strong dogs pulled each dogsled from the boat to the base camp.
3. Past tense verb	Carrying ten tons of supplies a day, the dogsleds helped set up the base camp.
4. Past participle	From the fully stocked base camp, Amundsen, four other men, and four dogsleds began the trek to the pole on October 14.
5. Plural possessive	Gliding over the ice, the dogsleds' progress was at first very rapid.
6. Comparative adjective	Soon a much harder part of the trip began; they had to cross a huge glacier.
7. Adverb made from adjective	The men finally crossed the glacier and again began rapid travel.
8. Plural noun	Once again the dogs moved quickly across the snow.

(continued)

Exercise 1 (continued) · Find It: Word Forms

Form	Sentence
9. Past tense	Amundsen worried that another explorer, Robert Scott, might beat him to the pole.
10. Superlative adjective	On December 14, 1911, Roald Amundsen and the four others became the happiest men on the planet; they reached the South Pole.

Exercise 2 · Choose It and Use It: Prefixes

▸ Read each pair of sentences.

▸ Look at the underlined word in the first sentence.

▸ Choose the prefix from the **Word Bank** that has the same meaning in the second sentence.

▸ Reread the second sentence with the newly created word.

Word Bank

pre	trans	inter	sub	anti	super

1. In 1869 the first railroad <u>across</u> the country was completed. It was the first

   _____ continental railroad.

2. The child did not have the strength to fight <u>against</u> the toxic infection. The

   doctors created an _____ toxin to stop the illness.

3. There was a discussion <u>between</u> the students in the class. It was an interesting

   _____ change.

4. Much is known about events that happened even <u>before</u> history was recorded.

   Fossils can tell us about _____ historic times.

5. Temperatures in the Antarctic are usually <u>below</u> freezing. They are

   _____ zero.

Exercise 3 · Rewrite It: Compound Sentences

▸ Read the text with your teacher.

▸ Reread the underlined sentences.

▸ Use a conjunction (**and, or, but**) to combine the underlined sentences into a compound sentence.

▸ Write the new compound sentence on the numbered line in the paragraph below.

▸ Check for sentence signals—capital letters, commas, and end punctuation.

▸ Reread the new paragraph with your teacher.

---

from "Mysteries of Antarctica"

Antarctica is big. It is cold, dry, and windy. Some plants and animals
<u>1</u>
such as krill can survive there. Krill are very small. They are food
<u>2</u>
for the largest mammal. Whales migrate to Antarctica in summer.
<u>2</u>   <u>3</u>
They eat the krill. As the winter begins, the large animals and birds
<u>3</u>
leave. The whales should swim north. They could be trapped in the
<u>4</u>
ice. The tiny life forms stay behind. They live inside the sea ice. They
<u>4</u>   <u>5</u>
wait for the next summer to start all over again.
<u>5</u>

Exercise 3 (continued) · Rewrite It: Compound Sentences

1._____

_____

Some plants and animals such as krill can survive there. **2.**_____

_____

_____

3._____

_____

As the winter begins, the large animals and birds leave. **4.**_____

_____

_____

The tiny life forms stay behind. **5.**_____

_____

_____

Resources

Resources

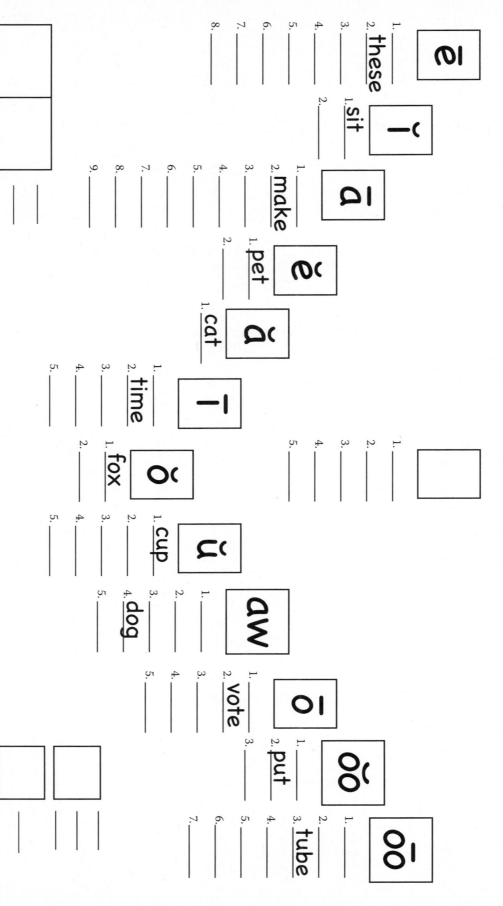

ē these

ĭ sit
1.
2.

ā make
1.
2.

ĕ pet
1.
2.

ă cat
1.
2.

ī time
1.
2.

ŏ fox
1.
2.

ŭ cup
1.
2.

aw dog
1.
2.
3.
4.
5.

ō vote
1.
2.

o͝o put
1.
2.
3.

o͞o tube
1.
2.

1.
2.
3.
4.
5.
6.
7.
8.

1.
2.
3.
4.
5.
6.
7.
8.
9.

1.
2.
3.
4.
5.

1.
2.
3.
4.
5.

1.
2.
3.
4.
5.

1.
2.
3.
4.
5.

1.
2.
3.
4.
5.
6.
7.

Consonant Chart

Mouth Position

Type of Consonant Sound	Lips	Lips/Teeth	Tongue Between Teeth	Tongue Behind Teeth	Roof of Mouth	Back of Mouth	Throat
Stops	/ b / / p /			/ t / / d /		/ k / / g /	
Fricatives		/ f / / v /	/ th / / <u>th</u> /	/ s / / z /	/ sh /		/ h /
Affricatives					/ j / / ch /		
Nasals	/ m /			/ n /		/ ng /	
Lateral				/ l /			
Semivowels	/ w / / hw /			/ r /	/ y /		

© Jane Fell Greene. Published by Sopris West Educational Services.
Adapted with permission from Bolinger, D. (1975). *Aspects of Language* (2nd ed.) (p. 41). New York: Harcourt Brace Jovanovich.

Divide It Checklist

Steps for Syllable Division	Example: disconnected
First, check the word for prefixes and suffixes. Circle them. Next, look at the rest of the word:	(dis)connect(ed)
1. Underline the **first** vowel. Write a **v** under it.	(dis)connect(ed)
2. Underline the **next** vowel. Write a **v** under it.	(dis)connect(ed)
3. Look at the letters **between** the vowels. Mark them with a **c** for consonant.	(dis)connect(ed) v c c v
4. Look at the pattern and divide according to the pattern.	(dis)con/nect(ed) v c c v
5. Place a diacritical mark over the vowels. Cross out the **e** at the end of final silent **e** syllables. Listen for schwa in the unaccented syllable, cross out the vowel, and place a ə symbol above it.	(dis)cŏn/nĕct(ed) v c c v
Finally, blend each syllable and read the word.	disconnected

Diacritical Marks and Symbols

Diacritical marks and **symbols** are used to indicate the correct sound for the vowel graphemes.

breve / brĕv /	ă	short vowel phonemes
macron	ā	long vowel phonemes
circumflex	âr	**r**-controlled phonemes
schwa	ə	schwa phoneme

Syllable Division Patterns

Pattern	How to Divide	Examples
vccv	vc / cv • Divide between the consonants. • The first syllable is closed. • The vowel sound is short.	năp/kĭn VCCV
vcv	v/cv • **Usually**, divide after the first vowel. • The first syllable is open. • The vowel sound is long. **Note:** If the first vowel is followed by an **r**, the syllable is **r**-controlled. or vc/v • If the first division does not result in a recognizable word, divide after the consonant. • The first syllable is closed. • The vowel sound is short.	sī/lĕnt VCV mâr/kĕt V CV nĕv/êr VCV
vcccv	• vc/ccv or vcc/cv • Divide before or after the blend or digraph. • Do not split the blend or digraph.	ăth/lēte VCCCV
vv	• v/v • Divide between the vowels if they are not a vowel team or diphthong. • The first syllable is open. • The vowel sound is long.	nē/ŏn V V
c + le	• /cle • Count back three and divide.	crā/dle 321

Word Fluency 1

	Correct	Errors
1st Try		
2nd Try		

lemon	melon	select	seven	second	salad	prison	punish	finish	vanish	10
seven	punish	vanish	select	finish	second	salad	lemon	prison	melon	20
select	finish	prison	punish	salad	melon	vanish	second	seven	lemon	30
second	salad	melon	vanish	lemon	finish	select	seven	punish	prison	40
vanish	select	finish	melon	punish	seven	prison	prison	lemon	salad	50
prison	seven	punish	salad	vanish	lemon	finish	melon	finish	select	60
salad	melon	lemon	finish	prison	select	seven	second	vanish	punish	70
melon	select	seven	prison	second	vanish	punish	finish	salad	lemon	80
punish	prison	salad	lemon	seven	melon	vanish	second	finish	second	90
lemon	melon	select	seven	second	salad	prison	punish	finish	vanish	100

Word Fluency 2

	Correct	Errors
1st Try		
2nd Try		

compact	complex	conduct	conflict	construct	consult	contact	content	subject	suspect	10
conflict	content	suspect	conduct	subject	construct	consult	compact	contact	complex	20
conduct	subject	contact	content	consult	complex	suspect	construct	conflict	compact	30
construct	consult	complex	suspect	compact	subject	conduct	conflict	content	contact	40
suspect	conduct	subject	complex	content	conflict	construct	contact	compact	consult	50
contact	conflict	content	consult	suspect	compact	subject	complex	construct	conduct	60
consult	complex	compact	subject	contact	conduct	conflict	construct	suspect	content	70
complex	conduct	conflict	contact	construct	subject	content	suspect	consult	compact	80
content	contact	consult	compact	conflict	conduct	complex	suspect	construct	subject	90
compact	complex	conduct	conflict	construct	consult	contact	content	subject	suspect	100

Unit 13 Fluency

Word Fluency 3

	Correct	Errors
1st Try		
2nd Try		

disconnect	uncommon	unplug	nonstop	nonfat	invent	instruct	distinct	disrupt	10
distinct	unlock	disrupt	nonfat	uncommon	instruct	disconnect	unplug	invent	20
disrupt	invent	nonstop	distinct	nonfat	unplug	unlock	uncommon	instruct	30
unlock	unplug	invent	instruct	invent	disrupt	disconnect	distinct	nonfat	40
nonstop	disrupt	nonfat	unlock	invent	unplug	invent	distinct	disconnect	50
instruct	nonfat	distinct	uncommon	disrupt	nonstop	instruct	uncommon	unplug	60
unplug	disconnect	nonfat	invent	instruct	unlock	instruct	disrupt	distinct	70
disrupt	nonstop	disconnect	unplug	nonfat	disconnect	invent	instruct	instruct	80
uncommon	nonfat	distinct	disconnect	invent	nonstop	disrupt	nonstop	unlock	90
disconnect	uncommon	unplug	unlock	nonfat	invent	instruct	distinct	disrupt	100

Word Fluency 4

#									
10	people	water	gone	most	people	see	most	water	look
20	look	most	see	water	look	gone	people	people	see
30	see	see	water	most	look	gone	people	see	water
40	people	water	gone	see	most	look	see	people	people
50	most	people	see	look	water	people	water	most	most
60	gone	look	water	people	see	most	look	people	water
70	people	water	gone	most	water	see	gone	most	look
80	water	see	look	people	water	look	people	look	see
90	gone	most	people	people	water	look	most	gone	most
100	most	look	water	people	most	people	most	look	gone

Unit 13 • Fluency **419**

Passage Fluency 1

<table>
<tr><td rowspan="2">Errors</td><td></td><td></td></tr>
<tr><td></td><td></td></tr>
<tr><td rowspan="2">Correct</td><td></td><td></td></tr>
<tr><td></td><td></td></tr>
<tr><td></td><td>1st Try</td><td>2nd Try</td></tr>
</table>

Some inventions were made just for fun. Some of them	10
are odd. Many of them have odd names. What do we	21
call inventions like these? They are "off-the-wall."	28
They are just not useful. Not many of them will sell.	39
They will not have any impact. They are not supposed	49
to! But many "off-the-wall" inventions have become	56
fads. A fad is a quick craze. Fads become the rage.	67
People like them. Fads are fun, but not for long.	77
Do you know someone who comes up with	85
"off-the-wall" inventions? Meet Mr. Robinson.	90
He has invented lots of nutty things. One of his	100
inventions stretches pasta! Another one puts a	107
square peg in a round hole! How useful is that? Are	118
you impressed? No. But you are amused. That's why	127
Mr. Robinson invents this nutty stuff. He just loves	136
tinkering. He loves odd things. Robinson is the king	145
of "off-the-wall" inventions!	148
Step back in time to 1985. In England, a man is	159
making a small 3-wheeled bike. This bike isn't	167
ridden. It's driven! It's called the C5. The C5 runs on	178
batteries, not gas. It emits no gas fumes. Lots of ships	189
use the C5. Why? The small C5s can drive across the	200
decks of big ships. A C5 helps move things on a ship.	212
But there is a problem. If you drive the C5 in traffic,	224
you'll find that it's too small. It's too sluggish. The	234
driver is too exposed. Passing cars emit gas fumes.	243
Drivers inhale the fumes!	247

Passage Fluency 2

	Correct	Errors
1st Try		
2nd Try		

What makes an inventor? Inventors have quick
minds. They think about problems. They come up
with solutions. Inventions impact our lives. How?
They make our lives better. Lots of us have ideas.
We think about things. If you have an invention,
you should get a patent. It says that your invention
belongs to you. It stops others from robbing your
idea.

Inventors begin with a problem. They think about
it. They think of the possibilities. Then, they find
a solution. This is how they think. Cars may be an
example. Cars use too much gas. The gas makes
fumes. The fumes pollute. Think about these
problems. What if you could make a car? Could a
car pollute less? Could a car use less gas? Is that
possible? It is. Here is one solution:

Make a car of plastic. That could solve it. The car
wouldn't be so heavy. It would use less gas. It would
pollute less. Plastic lasts. It doesn't rust. The color
doesn't fade. There would be a bonus, too. Plastic is
manmade. Think of all the juice we drink. It comes
in plastic jugs. We could use the same plastic. We
could make more cars. Is plastic the answer? Many
think so.

7
15
22
32
41
51
60
61

69
78
89
98
105
115
126
133

144
155
164
174
184
194
203
205

Word Fluency 1

	Correct	Errors
1st Try		
2nd Try		

#										
far	farm	star	start	part	park	spark	bar	barber	barn	10
park	spark	far	bar	star	farm	start	part	barn	barber	20
start	farm	star	far	spark	bar	park	barber	part	barn	30
far	park	barber	start	farm	star	barn	part	bar	spark	40
park	part	far	star	start	spark	barber	barn	farm	bar	50
part	farm	spark	barber	barn	park	start	bar	far	star	60
spark	barber	part	farm	park	start	star	far	barn	barber	70
far	bar	farm	start	barn	star	star	part	spark	park	80
part	barber	start	star	start	barn	barber	far	bar	spark	90
star	start	bar	barber	farm	spark	park	barn	part	far	100

Word Fluency 2

	Correct	Errors
1st Try		
2nd Try		

interpret	interact	understand	underbrush	interest	perhaps	person	permit	pepper	10
underbrush	perhaps	interpret	understand	person	underpass	interest	pepper	permit	20
underpass	interact	understand	interpret	underbrush	person	permit	interest	pepper	30
interpret	permit	interact	underpass	pepper	understand	interest	person	perhaps	40
underbrush	interpret	interest	understand	perhaps	permit	pepper	interact	person	50
interest	interact	perhaps	permit	underbrush	underpass	person	interpret	understand	60
perhaps	person	interest	pepper	underpass	understand	interpret	pepper	permit	70
interpret	permit	interact	pepper	understand	interest	person	perhaps	underbrush	80
interest	interact	understand	underbrush	pepper	permit	interpret	person	perhaps	90
understand	underpass	person	permit	interact	perhaps	underbrush	pepper	interest	interpret	100

Word Fluency 3

	Correct	Errors
1st Try		
2nd Try		

carve	horse	starve	nurse	forgive	serve	remorse	observe	verse	purse	10
horse	forgive	carve	serve	remorse	starve	verse	nurse	purse	observe	20
forgive	serve	observe	horse	verse	carve	purse	starve	remorse	nurse	30
observe	horse	remorse	carve	purse	nurse	serve	serve	nurse	starve	40
serve	verse	forgive	starve	horse	carve	nurse	purse	remorse	observe	50
verse	starve	horse	observe	serve	purse	forgive	remorse	carve	nurse	60
remorse	purse	starve	forgive	nurse	verse	remorse	observe	serve	observe	70
starve	nurse	serve	purse	carve	remorse	observe	forgive	horse	horse	80
forgive	verse	nurse	remorse	purse	observe	starve	horse	carve	starve	90
purse	starve	carve	nurse	remorse	serve	observe	verse	horse	forgive	100

Word Fluency 4

	Correct	Errors
1st Try		
2nd Try		

10	way	new	say	day	new	little	say	way	day	may
20	say	may	day	way	say	may	little	new	may	little
30	day	little	way	new	may	say	new	little	day	way
40	way	say	new	day	little	new	little	day	way	may
50	say	new	way	may	day	new	little	new	way	little
60	day	way	may	little	say	little	new	say	may	day
70	way	day	say	new	way	say	new	may	day	new
80	day	new	way	say	little	way	little	day	new	may
90	little	way	say	day	may	little	new	may	say	little
100	may	say	day	new	way	may	way	day	may	new

Passage Fluency 1

	Errors	
Correct		
1st Try		
2nd Try		

What do you do when you're bored? Some of us just | 11
sit and think. Others pick up a pen. If you have a pen, | 24
you might sketch. It feels natural. Everybody does | 32
it. Sketching is a basic form of art. Lines become | 42
shapes. Some shapes are abstract. Even you may | 50
not know what they are. Other shapes are concrete. | 59
Some of your shapes may turn into objects. Your | 68
pad gets filled with art. When you sketch, you're | 77
getting absorbed in art. You're expressing yourself by | 85
making art. | 87

The bell rings, and class begins. Everyone is sitting | 96
in a desk. Others begin to take notes. You begin to | 107
sketch. Your lines become art. Your name becomes | 115
art. The sun comes up—on your paper. Stars appear. | 125
But what happens when it's time for the test? Where | 135
are your notes? Notes will help you pass the test. | 145
Sketches won't. It's hard to sketch and take notes at | 155
the same time! | 158

Meet Keron Grant. He was born in Jamaica in 1976. | 168
As a kid, he liked sketching. He liked comics. He | 178
loved The Hulk®. He started sketching Hulk. He | 186
sketched Hulk hundreds of times. When he was 14, | 195
he came to the USA. He visited a comic book store. | 206
Then he got fired up! He began sketching the figures. | 216
Today, his figures are in comic books. Iron Man was | 226
one of his creations. Keron's sketches led him to | 235
success. | 236

	Correct	Errors
1st Try		
2nd Try		

Fame was in store for Elisa Kleven. She made a   10
name for herself. It began when she was a little girl.   21
Common scraps fascinated her. She used scraps to   29
make art. Nutshells became beds. Caps from drinks   37
became small baking pans. She loved to make little   46
settings. Elisa's settings inspired her. She began to   54
tell little tales. Her tales led to books for children.   64
Next, Elisa's scraps became 3-D art in her books.   73
Yarn made a horse's mane. Twine made a   81
first-rate bird's nest. Bits of colored rags made   89
a dozen different shapes. Elisa had discovered   96
something. Common scraps can make fantastic art.   103

The first form of art was cave art. Cave artists made   114
lots of sketches inside caves. Caves protected the art.   123
Wind didn't hurt it. Water didn't wash it off. The sun   134
didn't fade it. A hundred tales are told in cave art.   145
Cave art tells the tales of the lives of cave people. The   157
cave dwellers hunted. They fished. They sketched   164
crude maps. They made messages for each other. The   173
art they made is still there. The messages they left   183
us tell us much. From cave art, we learn history. We   194
learn about the lives of some of the first humans. We   205
learn something even more important. We learn that   213
humans have always been obsessed with making art.   221

Word Fluency 1

	Correct	Errors
1st Try		
2nd Try		

10	detect	fever	poem	silent	music	secret	moment	diet	equip	acorn
20	fever	detect	secret	equip	moment	diet	poem	acorn	music	silent
30	detect	secret	fever	poem	silent	music	acorn	diet	equip	moment
40	music	poem	secret	diet	detect	equip	moment	fever	silent	acorn
50	poem	equip	detect	moment	fever	music	diet	acorn	secret	silent
60	diet	acorn	poem	music	silent	fever	moment	diet	music	secret
70	fever	detect	acorn	diet	moment	silent	silent	acorn	poem	music
80	silent	music	poem	secret	detect	diet	detect	secret	equip	acorn
90	music	poem	acorn	fever	silent	moment	diet	fever	moment	secret
100	acorn	secret	detect	silent	music	equip	fever	equip	poem	diet

Word Fluency 2

	Correct	Errors
1st Try		
2nd Try		

tornado	tornado	undergo	tuxedo	menu	videos	heroes	zeroes	ago	10
videos	heroes	tornado	zeroes	undergo	tornado	tuxedo	menu	ago	goes	20
tuxedo	tornado	undergo	tornado	heroes	zeroes	videos	goes	menu	ago	30
tornado	videos	goes	tuxedo	tornado	undergo	ago	menu	zeroes	heroes	40
videos	menu	tornado	undergo	tuxedo	heroes	goes	ago	tornado	zeroes	50
menu	tornado	heroes	goes	ago	videos	tuxedo	zeroes	tornado	undergo	60
heroes	zeroes	menu	tornado	videos	tuxedo	undergo	tornado	ago	goes	70
tornado	goes	tuxedo	ago	undergo	menu	zeroes	heroes	videos	80
menu	tornado	tuxedo	undergo	videos	ago	goes	tornado	zeroes	heroes	90
undergo	tuxedo	zeroes	goes	tornado	heroes	videos	ago	menu	tornado	100

Word Fluency 3

	Correct	Errors
1st Try		
2nd Try		

10	supersonic	superstar	prevent	preset	predict	menu	tuxedo	undergo	report	result
20	superstar	supersonic	menu	tuxedo	report	undergo	prevent	result	preset	predict
30	supersonic	menu	superstar	predict	prevent	preset	report	undergo	result	tuxedo
40	preset	prevent	menu	supersonic	undergo	report	superstar	predict	superstar	result
50	prevent	report	supersonic	superstar	preset	superstar	tuxedo	menu	menu	predict
60	undergo	result	prevent	tuxedo	predict	supersonic	preset	report	report	menu
70	superstar	supersonic	report	undergo	tuxedo	predict	result	prevent	prevent	preset
80	predict	preset	prevent	menu	supersonic	undergo	tuxedo	superstar	superstar	result
90	preset	prevent	report	superstar	predict	result	preset	report	result	menu
100	report	menu	supersonic	predict	preset	result	superstar	prevent	tuxedo	undergo

Word Fluency 4

Correct	Errors
1st Try	
2nd Try	

through	though	right	good	great	year	through	great	right	year	**10**
though	good	great	through	right	though	good	year	great	right	**20**
through	year	good	though	good	through	year	though	through	though	**30**
right	good	though	great	through	year	though	great	right	year	**40**
good	through	right	great	through	good	great	though	through	through	**50**
year	though	good	right	year	right	through	great	though	right	**60**
though	good	through	year	great	year	good	through	though	though	**70**
year	great	though	right	through	year	year	right	good	good	**80**
right	though	great	through	year	good	though	year	year	great	**90**
through	good	though	right	great	year	through	though	great	through	**100**

Passage Fluency 1

	Correct	Errors
1st Try		
2nd Try		

They fill comic strips. They have superhuman skills. 8
They're strong, quick, talented, and wise. They 15
ensure that good wins over evil. Who are these 24
superhumans? Superheroes! We all love heroes. 30
Heroes can inspire us. They can give us hope. 39

Humans wanted to make sense of their world. They 48
wanted to understand its order. They wanted to 56
understand its origin. They strived to understand its 64
conflicts. They made up tales to explain their world. 73
These tales are called myths. Myths are just made-up 82
tales, but people used to believe them. People lived 91
their lives as if myths were based in fact. In these 102
tales, different gods ruled over the world. 109

Long ago, the Romans told about the gods in their 119
myths. Saturn was one of their gods. He was the god 130
of time. Saturn had three sons. They were Jupiter, 139
Neptune, and Pluto. Jupiter ruled the air. Jupiter was 148
the king of the gods. He was the strongest god. Juno 159
was Jupiter's wife. She was the goddess of husbands 168
and wives. Neptune ruled the seas. He gave the waves 178
white caps. He made the waters still. He held the fate 189
of ships in his hands. A trip could be safe or unsafe. 201
It was Neptune's choice. His brother, Pluto, ruled 209
over the dead. His kingdom was a dark and grim 219
land. It was filled with evil. Pluto ruled over all who 230
entered his kingdom. He ushered the dead into the 239
afterlife. These myths are still told. The stories are 248
still exciting. But nobody believes them anymore. 255

Correct	Errors
1st Try	
2nd Try	

Not every hero is a superhero. For some, it's a job. 11
Some spend their lives helping others. Think of 19
firefighters. Think of soldiers. Think of the police. 27
These are the unsung heroes. They risk their lives. 36

No matter where you live, fire is a big problem. 46
Firefighters save lives. What happens when a home 54
catches fire? A call to 911 is a call to save lives. It's 67
your direct line to the unsung heroes. What happens 76
when a forest catches fire? Fires burn huge plots of 86
land. They kill birds and plants. Enter the unsung 95
heroes. They put out the fires. 101

Men and women join the military. When they do, 110
they put their lives on the line. They protect us. They 121
watch over the homelands. Sometimes, war breaks 128
out. They are called to protect and defend. No matter 138
what the issue, some people support it, and others 147
reject it. It is hard to do your job when many people 159
do not support you. Yet our soldiers do their jobs and 170
expect nothing in return. We should have pride in 179
them. They deserve their country's thanks. They, too, 187
are unsung heroes. 190

Crime is a big problem. Some people shoplift. Some 199
use drugs. Some are reckless drivers. Some harm 207
others. The police are there to help. They bring back 217
order. They help solve crimes. Their work makes our 226
lives safer. Like soldiers and firefighters, they are 234
unsung heroes. 236

Word Fluency 1

	Correct	Errors
1st Try		
2nd Try		

became	beside	define	debate	finite	demote	migrate	locate	polite	describe	10
locate	migrate	became	demote	define	beside	debate	finite	describe	polite	20
debate	beside	define	became	migrate	locate	demote	polite	finite	describe	30
became	demote	polite	debate	beside	define	describe	finite	locate	migrate	40
locate	finite	became	define	migrate	debate	polite	describe	beside	demote	50
finite	beside	migrate	polite	describe	demote	debate	locate	became	define	60
migrate	locate	finite	beside	demote	debate	define	became	describe	polite	70
became	polite	beside	debate	describe	define	finite	locate	migrate	demote	80
finite	beside	debate	define	locate	describe	polite	became	demote	migrate	90
define	debate	locate	polite	beside	migrate	demote	describe	finite	became	100

	Correct	Errors
1st Try		
2nd Try		

athlete	complete	compute	admire	inside	include	provide	promote	presume	describe	10
promote	provide	athlete	include	compute	complete	admire	inside	describe	presume	20
admire	complete	compute	athlete	provide	promote	include	presume	inside	describe	30
athlete	include	presume	admire	complete	compute	describe	inside	promote	provide	40
promote	inside	athlete	compute	include	provide	presume	describe	complete	admire	50
inside	complete	provide	presume	describe	include	admire	promote	athlete	compute	60
provide	promote	inside	complete	include	admire	compute	athlete	describe	presume	70
athlete	presume	complete	include	describe	compute	inside	promote	provide	admire	80
inside	complete	admire	compute	promote	describe	presume	athlete	include	provide	90
compute	admire	promote	presume	complete	provide	include	describe	inside	athlete	100

Word Fluency 3

	Correct	Errors
1st Try		
2nd Try		

arrive	comprise	dispose	impose	passive	positive	primitive	repetitive	promise	purchase	10
repetitive	primitive	arrive	positive	dispose	comprise	impose	passive	purchase	promise	20
impose	comprise	dispose	arrive	primitive	repetitive	positive	promise	passive	purchase	30
arrive	positive	promise	impose	comprise	dispose	purchase	passive	repetitive	primitive	40
repetitive	passive	arrive	dispose	positive	primitive	promise	purchase	comprise	impose	50
passive	comprise	primitive	promise	purchase	positive	impose	repetitive	arrive	dispose	60
primitive	repetitive	passive	comprise	positive	impose	dispose	arrive	purchase	promise	70
arrive	promise	comprise	positive	purchase	dispose	passive	repetitive	primitive	impose	80
passive	comprise	impose	dispose	repetitive	purchase	promise	arrive	positive	primitive	90
dispose	impose	repetitive	promise	comprise	primitive	positive	purchase	passive	arrive	100

Word Fluency 4

	Correct	Errors
1st Try		
2nd Try		

want	work	today	tomorrow	sound	again	today	tomorrow	again	10
work	want	sound	today	again	want	tomorrow	work	tomorrow	20
again	sound	today	work	sound	work	again	today	want	30
today	tomorrow	sound	again	work	want	tomorrow	today	sound	40
again	want	tomorrow	sound	today	again	sound	today	again	50
want	work	today	tomorrow	again	sound	work	today	tomorrow	60
sound	again	tomorrow	today	work	sound	again	tomorrow	want	70
work	today	want	sound	again	tomorrow	today	want	sound	80
today	sound	work	again	today	tomorrow	sound	work	tomorrow	90
again	want	tomorrow	today	want	sound	tomorrow	work	again	100

Passage Fluency 1

	Correct	Errors
1st Try		
2nd Try		

One person can make things happen. Shriver did.   8
She began in 1963. She began a summer day camp.   18
She held the camp at her home. She invited athletes   28
like Steven. She watched them compete in sports.   36
She saw their desire to win. They worked hard.   45
She planned events. There were games. There was   53
swimming and track. Competing was a thrill! They   61
loved it. They were happy. Shriver saw them smile.   70
She made up her mind. In 1968, her camp became   80
Special Olympics. The games grew. More people   87
came. By 1987, all 50 states sent athletes. Now,   96
Special Olympics is important in the lives of many   104
people. Today, there are 26 sports. There are summer   113
and winter sports. From all over the world, athletes   122
come to take part in the games. These athletes   132
compete at no cost. How are the games funded?   141
Shriver has used grants. Many have donated. Many   149
others have made money with events. You can help,   157
too. Get started! Help fund Special Olympics!   166
  168

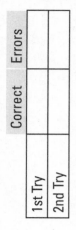

Some athletes love risks. They do their sport. They   9
add a twist. Extreme sports have added risks.   18
Athletes get a thrill. Skating is an example. Extreme   26
skaters are fine athletes. They love the risk. For them,   36
it's fun.   38

Extreme skaters use in-line skates. They're not like   46
skates of the past. They're new. They're light. They're   55
fast. They're strong. Skaters don't use skating rinks.   63
They use skate parks. Skate parks have ramps.   71
Skaters even have a jargon. They have their own   80
words. Take the top of the ramp. It has a name.   91
It's the "coping." It's where they do tricks. They do   101
amazing jumps. They twist. They turn. They spend   109
lots of time practicing. They start with small tricks.   118
First, there's the crossover. They just cross one skate   127
over the other. Then they add things. They practice.   136
They get better. This takes time. They get better.   145
Then, they try bashing. That means going down   153
steps. Sometimes, there's no skate park. They go   161
somewhere else. They use steps. They use parking   169
lots. They even use curbs. They really take skating to   179
the next level!   182

Extreme athletes protect themselves. They use   188
helmets. They use pads. Still, they can be injured.   197
Without protection, skaters get hurt. They can miss   205
a landing. They can lose control. Extreme athletes   213
are risk-takers. They love to compete. They take their   222
sport to a new level. But they think of safety, too.   233
They have to. They have fun. But they always take   243
care. They're safe athletes.   247

Word Fluency 1

	Correct	Errors
1st Try		
2nd Try		

10	why	sky	fly	imply	deny	rely	try	dry	by	my
20	sky	rely	why	by	dry	fly	my	imply	deny	try
30	why	dry	sky	try	imply	by	fly	rely	my	deny
40	fly	sky	by	why	rely	dry	deny	my	try	imply
50	by	why	dry	my	deny	sky	try	imply	fly	rely
60	dry	by	deny	why	my	imply	fly	rely	sky	try
70	my	deny	try	fly	dry	why	by	sky	rely	imply
80	rely	why	my	sky	imply	try	deny	fly	dry	by
90	deny	my	why	try	rely	sky	dry	imply	by	fly
100	why	rely	try	dry	deny	my	fly	by	imply	sky

Word Fluency 2

	Correct	Errors
1st Try		
2nd Try		

candy	copy	penny	army	tiny	thirty	baby	body	story	happy	**10**
penny	baby	candy	body	copy	story	army	happy	tiny	thirty	**20**
baby	army	penny	copy	candy	tiny	body	thirty	story	happy	**30**
copy	tiny	baby	army	penny	happy	candy	story	thirty	body	**40**
body	story	tiny	thirty	baby	copy	penny	army	candy	happy	**50**
army	thirty	story	baby	tiny	happy	body	copy	penny	candy	**60**
tiny	body	army	penny	story	happy	candy	happy	copy	copy	**70**
thirty	baby	penny	happy	happy	candy	copy	story	army	body	**80**
baby	candy	copy	tiny	story	thirty	penny	thirty	happy	army	**90**
story	tiny	baby	candy	thirty	army	happy	body	copy	penny	**100**

Word Fluency 3

	Correct	Errors
1st Try		
2nd Try		

#									
10	pretty	quickly	bye	eye	system	type	gym	comply	supply
20	system	pretty	gym	comply	property	supply	quickly	bye	type
30	gym	quickly	property	type	comply	system	bye	eye	eye
40	property	type	pretty	bye	gym	supply	quickly	eye	comply
50	pretty	quickly	system	supply	eye	type	bye	quickly	gym
60	system	pretty	eye	quickly	comply	gym	bye	supply	property
70	pretty	quickly	comply	property	bye	type	gym	property	comply
80	comply	pretty	type	bye	supply	property	eye	quickly	system
90	gym	bye	supply	property	system	property	supply	eye	quickly
100	supply	pretty	bye	quickly	type	property	gym	system	eye

Word Fluency 4

	Correct	Errors
1st Try		
2nd Try		

10	20	30	40	50	60	70	80	90	100
laugh	engine	laugh	certain	answer	certain	engine	laugh	answer	certain
poor	answer	engine	laugh	poor	engine	oil	answer	poor	engine
engine	laugh	answer	engine	laugh	answer	laugh	certain	engine	laugh
answer	certain	oil	poor	engine	poor	answer	poor	laugh	poor
laugh	poor	answer	certain	certain	oil	poor	answer	certain	oil
oil	laugh	engine	laugh	engine	poor	laugh	certain	engine	certain
poor	oil	poor	answer	poor	certain	answer	answer	oil	poor
answer	poor	engine	laugh	answer	engine	oil	poor	answer	engine
certain	engine	laugh	engine	poor	laugh	certain	engine	answer	certain
engine	answer	certain	poor	laugh	answer	engine	laugh	laugh	answer

Passage Fluency 1

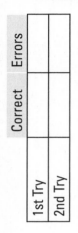

	Errors	
Correct		
	1st Try	2nd Try

Solve this puzzle. Its base is flat. It has four corners. 11
It has four sides. The sides slope up. The top isn't flat. 23
It has a sharp tip. It was made long ago. It's huge. It's 36
in Egypt. About 90 remain. You figured it out. It's a 47
pyramid! And it's amazing! 51

Why were they constructed? They had two basic 59
uses. First, they were sacred sites. Rites were held 68
inside. Second, they were final resting sites. They 76
were the graves of kings. 81

The pyramids were constructed long ago. There were 89
no motors. There were no cranes. Workers didn't even 98
have a wheel! It seems like an impossible task. The 108
stones were huge. They made huge numbers of blocks. 117
One base block was big. It weighed 15 tons. How did 128
they do it? Their method involved steps. First, they 137
dug the stone. Then, it was put on a raft. The raft 149
drifted down the Nile River. At the site, the stone was 160
taken off. Workers chipped and shaped. They sculpted. 168
They carved a channel into the stone. Next, they drove 178
a wooden wedge into it. They drenched the wedge in 188
water. It expanded. They added more water. The wedge 197
expanded more. At last, the stone split. Then they 206
cut it. They used chisels. They used stone hammers. 215
They got it into the desired shape. Up the ramps it 226
went. The pyramid rose. So did the ramps. Stones 235
were dragged up the sides. Block stacked upon block. 244
Finally, they reached the top. They put on a capstone. 254
It was finished. One more amazing pyramid! 261

	Correct	Errors
1st Try		
2nd Try		

Visualize yourself in a different place. Think of 8
yourself in ancient times. Think about living in 16
Egypt. It was an interesting time. Surprisingly, life 24
was similar to life today. Some customs were the 33
same. People had jobs. They had activities. Their 41
lifestyles were similar. Let's go back in time. We'll 50
meet two students. 53

First, meet Moses. He's a farmer's son. In Egypt, 62
the public depends on farmers. They supply all the 71
crops. At harvest time, Moses helps his dad. He 80
gathers crops. Sometimes, he covers them to protect 88
them. His father hopes the crops will be plentiful. 97
If so, there will be more work. The crops have to be 109
stored. Moses' dad cannot farm the land from June 118
to September. The Nile River floods in these months. 127
Their lands are covered with water. When the river 136
floods, they still have to work. Farmers take other 145
jobs. Many work on the pyramids. When the river 154
gets back to normal, so do they. They return home. 164
Life on the farm begins again. 170

Hebeny studies hard. Her father is a scribe. His job 180
has extreme value in Egypt. It is the one job that 191
requires a formal education. The writing is done 199
with a code. The code has no letters. It uses symbols. 210
These represent ideas. Most scribes are men. But 218
Hebeny wants to master the skills. She wants to 227
become a scribe. She wants to be like her dad. 237

Word Fluency 1

	Correct	Errors
1st Try		
2nd Try		

10	why	direct	diet	report	remote	line	try	alone	short	sharp
20	direct	line	why	short	alone	diet	sharp	report	remote	try
30	why	alone	direct	try	report	short	diet	remote	sharp	line
40	diet	direct	short	why	remote	alone	line	sharp	try	report
50	short	why	alone	sharp	line	direct	try	report	diet	remote
60	alone	short	remote	why	sharp	report	direct	line	direct	try
70	sharp	line	try	diet	report	line	why	short	direct	report
80	remote	sharp	sharp	direct	sharp	why	try	try	alone	short
90	line	why	why	try	why	direct	alone	diet	report	short
100	why	remote	try	alone	line	sharp	diet	short	report	direct

1st Try	2nd Try
Correct	
Errors	

Words									#
contest	contact	pretend	translate	transport	something	sometimes	sunset	sunrise	10
pretend	something	contest	sometimes	contact	sunset	prevent	translate	transport	20
something	prevent	pretend	contact	contest	translate	sometimes	sunset	sunrise	30
contact	translate	something	prevent	sunrise	pretend	contest	transport	sometimes	40
sometimes	sunset	translate	transport	something	contact	contest	prevent	sunrise	50
prevent	transport	sunset	something	translate	sunrise	sometimes	pretend	contest	60
translate	sometimes	prevent	sunset	pretend	something	contest	sunrise	contact	70
transport	something	translate	sunrise	prevent	contest	contact	sunset	sometimes	80
something	contest	contact	translate	sometimes	transport	pretend	sunrise	prevent	90
sunset	translate	something	contest	transport	prevent	sunrise	contact	pretend	100

Word Fluency 3

	Correct	Errors
1st Try		
2nd Try		

again	certain	gone	laugh	poor	they	bye	though	today	tomorrow	10
laugh	bye	though	again	today	certain	they	gone	tomorrow	poor	20
they	again	bye	poor	certain	tomorrow	laugh	today	though	gone	30
certain	poor	they	though	again	bye	gone	today	laugh	today	40
gone	today	certain	bye	they	again	again	poor	though	tomorrow	50
laugh	bye	again	laugh	gone	certain	though	poor	they	poor	60
again	they	poor	laugh	bye	gone	certain	today	though	tomorrow	70
poor	gone	though	they	today	again	bye	laugh	tomorrow	certain	80
laugh	though	they	certain	tomorrow	poor	again	bye	gone	gone	90
they	poor	gone	today	laugh	though	certain	bye	tomorrow	again	100

Word Fluency 4

	Correct	Errors
1st Try		
2nd Try		

who	want	what	answer	people	there	their	two	too	to	10
there	who	two	people	too	want	to	what	answer	their	20
two	what	want	their	who	too	there	answer	to	people	30
want	their	who	two	answer	to	what	people	there	too	40
who	what	there	to	people	their	answer	too	want	two	50
there	who	people	to	what	too	want	to	answer	their	60
who	what	to	what	people	there	their	people	there	to	70
too	too	want	two	answer	to	want	there	who	there	80
two	answer	to	their	want	there	who	too	what	their	90
to	who	answer	too	what	their	want	two	there	people	100

Passage Fluency 1

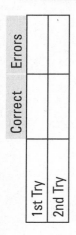

Correct	Errors
1st Try	
2nd Try	

The temperature is less than zero! The wind gusts at 10
more than 200 mph. The wind chill hits the danger 20
zone. The land is frozen. Welcome to Antarctica. It 29
is also called the South Pole. It is very dry and cold. 41
There's not much life. Small plants live on the frozen 51
shore. Krill thrive in the cold waters. Whales migrate 60
to the Antarctic. They come just for krill. Other 69
forms of life come. Many birds visit too. 77

At the pole, days are far from normal. In the summer, 88
there is constant day. It is never dark. Summer 97
begins in October. It ends in March! These are 106
winter months in the U.S. The planet tilts. This 115
brings constant sunshine. Is it hard to go to bed? 125
Yes. The sun is still up. Dwellings have thick shades. 135
This makes it dark inside. What is it like in winter? 146
It is dark all the time! The planet tilts. This prevents 157
direct sunshine. It's hard to get up in the dark. An 168
alarm clock wakes you, not the rising sun. There is 178
some light in the sky. It comes from gases. Swirling 188
gases color the winter sky. To adjust takes time! 197

People do not make the Antarctic their home. They 206
come for a short time. They study. They write. They 216
work to uncover secrets. Secrets from the past unlock 225
the future. 227

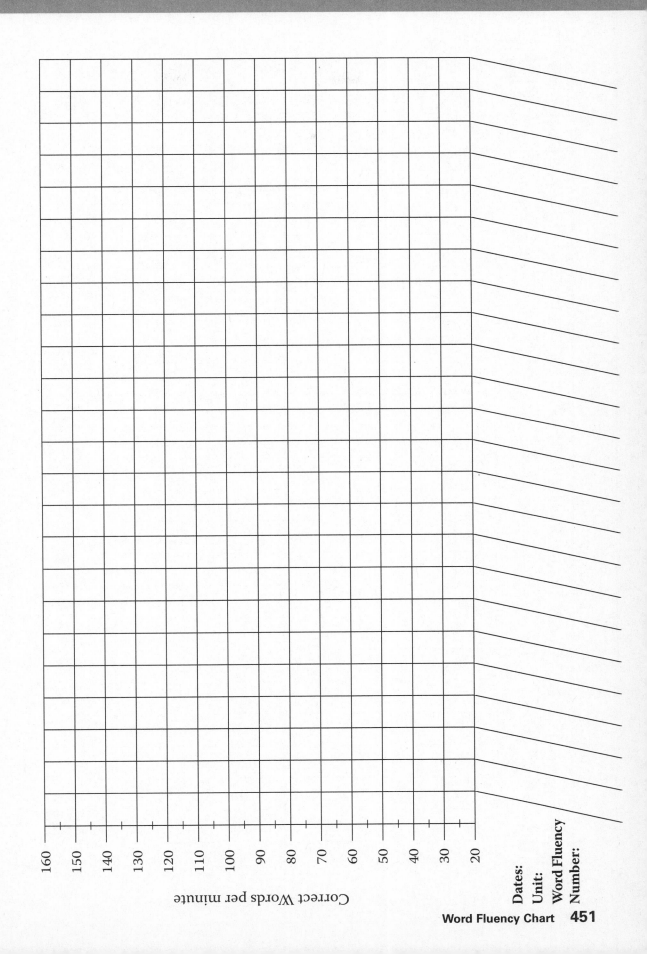

Word Fluency Chart

Correct Words per minute

160 150 140 130 120 110 100 90 80 70 60 50 40 30 20

Dates:
Unit:
Word Fluency
Number:

Fluency Charts

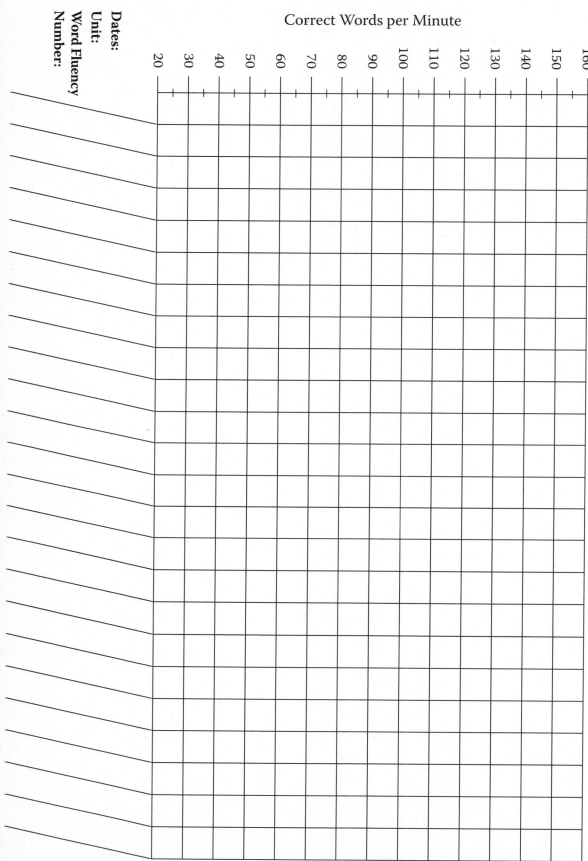

Correct Words per Minute

160 150 140 130 120 110 100 90 80 70 60 50 40 30 20

Dates:
Unit:
Word Fluency
Number:

Correct Phrases Per _____

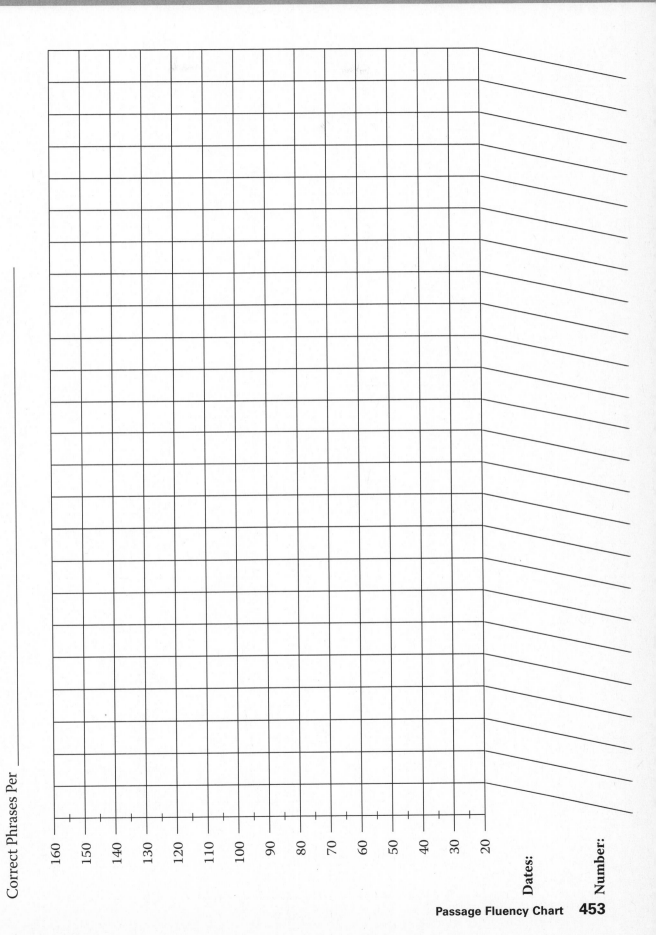

160

150

140

130

120

110

100

90

80

70

60

50

40

30

20

Dates:

Number:

Unit 13

gone	look	most
people	see	water

Unit 14

day	little	may
new	say	way

Essential Word Cards

Unit 15

good	great	right
though	through	year

Unit 16

again	sound	today
tomorrow	want	work

Unit 17

answer	certain	engine
laugh	oil	poor

Word Building Letter Cards

a	a	b	b	c	c	d
d	f	f	g	g	h	h
i	i	j	j	k	k	l
l	m	m	n	n	o	o
p	p	qu	qu	r	r	s
s	t	t	v	v	w	w
x	x	y	y	z	z	ck
ck	ll	ll	ss	ss	ff	ff
zz	zz	ar	er	ir	or	ur

Word Building Letter Cards

D	C	C	B	B	A	A
H	H	G	G	F	F	D
L	K	K	J	J	I	I
O	O	N	N	M	M	L
S	R	R	Qu	Qu	P	P
W	W	V	V	T	T	S
	Z	Z	Y	Y	X	X

Student _____ Date_____

Syllable Types

Bank It

Prefixes

Bank It

Student _____ Date_____

Prefixes

Bank It

Student _____ Date _____

Suffixes
